Splinters in the Quick

Other books by Ronald E. Sleeth

Persuasive Preaching, 1956
Proclaiming the Word, 1964
Which Way to God? 1968

Splinters in the Quick

RONALD E. SLEETH

WORD BOOKS, Publisher
Waco, Texas · London, England

For
Molly and Tom
two critics-in-residence

Contents

Introduction 9

Unidentified Objects 15

"What's in a Name?" 29

Anyone for Shepherding? 43

Tragedy and Triumph 57

Two Minutes Till Midnight 71

And the Walls Came Tumbling Down 83

The Last Word 93

The Lost Parable 105

One Thing Is Needed 115

Jesus and the Generation Gap 127

Introduction

There are those who claim that you cannot print a sermon. Since I have been one who has argued for that point of view, this reasoning naturally has some validity for me. The contention is that since a sermon is an *event* (or perhaps in our day, a "happening"), you cannot print that experience. You can publish an abstract of the sermon—but not the sermon itself, for it is an encounter between preacher and people, God and preacher, people and God, people and people. This is to say nothing about the importance of the Holy Spirit in the service, or about the nonverbal and nonrational aspects of preaching which are invariably important in the art of proclamation, but are hardly conducive to printing in a book. How, then, do you publish a sermon, let alone a whole book of them?

Although I still feel that much of the reasoning against printing sermons is sound, I nevertheless am

publishing several selected sermons for two com-
pelling reasons. The first is professional and the
second is personal. First of all, Dr. Paul Scherer in
The Word God Sent wrote a book in which the first
part was theory and the last was a group of sermons
to illustrate or confirm his theory. I admired both his
courage and competence. Even though I make no
comparisons of my work with Dr. Scherer's, except to
acknowledge publicly what a great mentor he has
been to many of us, it does seem plausible that a
theorist of preaching should be obliged to be judged
by his practice as well as by his theory. In other places
—and through years of teaching—I have developed
what I consider to be an adequate theory of preaching. Here it is my concern to dramatize that theory
with some actual sermons.

The second reason for the book is more personal.
Several years ago when visiting a revered teacher of
English, I was perplexed to discover among his vast
library a considerable number of books of sermons.
When I expressed my surprise, he confessed that he
had lived most of his life in a small college town and
after listening to the usual preaching fare to be expected in such a situation, it was these books which had
fed him spiritually all through the years. I am sure now
that many people, both clergy and laity, are in the
same position. There are those who find spiritual
meaning in reading others' sermons, and somehow
even the nonrational dimensions mentioned earlier in

connection with the preaching event come through to them in the pages of a book. In short, not every purchaser and reader of books of sermons is a homiletic Shylock hoping to carve his pound of flesh from someone else's carcass.

There has been no endeavor to include these sermons under a single unifying theme. They represent Christian affirmations—essentially biblical—with relevant adaptation to our common experiences. This is what preaching, indeed what Christianity should aim to be. It is an incarnational act of the Word becoming flesh in the world in which we all live. These sermons seek to do this and if a theme is sought, it probably could be found in refuting the oft-repeated suspicion that God is neither alive nor very active. These sermons affirm that he is very active, alive, and concerned for both our world and our individual lives.

One other thing: These are not "closet" sermons. (Playwrights have often written "closet" dramas which are plays not to be acted out but simply to be read as literature.) These sermons were all oral presentations and are not literary creations. An endeavor has been made to correct the infelicities without destroying the oral style.

Acknowledgments should be made to the *Peabody Reflector* and *The Pulpit* for two of the sermons which have already appeared in print. "Two Minutes Till Midnight" was printed in both publications and "Tragedy and Triumph" appeared in the latter. A careful reader will see that I have made use of *The Interpreter's Bible* as well as other exegetical tools. I have tried to show that the extensive resources available to the preacher can actually be used, but I have kept footnotes and citations hidden in the back so the sermons will be just that. My colleague, Decherd Turner, read the manuscript and Mrs. Anne Norris typed it.

Dallas, 1970   RONALD E. SLEETH

Unidentified
Objects

Unidentified Objects

In Arthur Miller's play, *Death of a Salesman,* we see in microcosm one of our deepest problems. This problem is man's concern (or unconcern) to discover who he really is. Willy Loman is a salesman who never has had this self-knowledge. He has had an image of himself and his sons as "well-liked" and "successful." Even in suicide at the end of the play there is no assurance that Willy has seen himself as he is—a failure. His son, Biff, a loafer whom Willy has filled with "hot air" as being "great," finally comes to the realization of his identity as a phony. He sums up his father's life at the cemetery at the end of the play when he remarks to Willy's best friend: "Charley, the man didn't know who he was."[1]

What a sad epitaph!

I.

In one degree or another all of us are involved in discovering who we are. The problem of identity is a problem for all of us, and we are all in danger of having Willy's epitaph become ours. Life and maturity are concerned with self-discovery and self-identity. All of us are searching for that real "me." This is part of our maturing. It is part of the questions which confront us: Who are we? Why are we here? Where are we going?

In our questioning lies the heritage of man. The animal cannot ask who he is. The slave does not need to know who he is. His limits of self-identity are set. The same is true of a person whose identity is set by society and by his place in it—by his caste. We are told that the disintegration of the caste system in the Eastern world, particularly in India, has brought new need for self-identity. Only a creative individual can ask these questions—and for him questioning is a must. Our educational institutions are, in part, based on the assumption that as students we are seeking to know who we really are. In short, self-discovery is at the center of our being and of our beliefs.

Now this is not to say that everyone wants to know who he really is. We are so often afraid of that knowledge. We desire to keep the central core of our "self" untouched. I am not sure I will be happy with the real "me." I might discover that what I am really like is quite different from the image I try to project, and this revelation would be frightening. If I discover the weakness of the real me, how can I accept myself and those weaknesses? The real "me" may be quite different from the person I pretend to be.

The result is that we try to protect our identity. One way we do this is to cover the core of self with intellectualizations and verbalizations. This not only keeps us from seeing the true self, but also discourages others from knowing us. It is difficult for two people to enter into a deep relationship with each other until they can get behind the façade of the verbal. The verbal becomes a last-ditch defense against the castle of our souls.

We can see also this fear of revealing one's core of being in romance. Romance—often opposed to love—is based upon deception. (Some cynic might suggest that the cosmetic industry testifies to this fact.) Our best foot is forward. Very seldom do I—short of engagement—desire to reveal to my favorite girl all of the real me. I might get involved. I might get hurt. She would know too much. Part of the "game" is to permit her to see only the image I wish to project. No doubt that is why there is disillusionment when the prom music fades away and the dirty dishes fill the sink.

Now it is not only difficult to tell who we are ourselves; it is equally difficult to find out who anyone else is as well. We live in a world of labels, of packaged products, of people who are really unidentified objects in spite of all the names we attach to them. How difficult it is to know the real personality even of our friends. We refer to each other as Dekes, or Kappas, Democrats, Republicans, liberals, segregationists, conservatives, fundamentalists, hippies. These labels obscure the real "me" in any person—ourselves included. How convenient these labels—and how concealing! How difficult to get through these labels to know someone, even ourselves.

Our problem, then, is one of identity—knowing who we really are. We want to know and yet we don't. Still, we find that if we can't be ourselves authentically, then we can't know ourselves truly—and certainly not any one else.

How, then, can we find out who we are?

II.

The Christian faith has always affirmed that we know ourselves in relationship to God—when we have known him we know ourselves. Knowing him, we find acceptance for the way we are rather than the way we seem to be. We can be ourselves. And the moment we have been accepted it is true that we have new responsibilities, but we also have a new freedom—freedom to become ourselves.

For the Christian, this knowledge of God is more than accepting an abstract principle of God's existence. It is more than worship of a purposeful principle. Knowledge of God is recognition of and obedience to One who has acted purposefully in the world. And the important thing about the knowledge of God is that we can know God only as he chooses to reveal himself. We can know objects or principles on our own initiative, but we can know persons only if they choose to reveal themselves. This God has done in creation, in man himself, and above all in his Son, Jesus Christ.

In other words, to know God, one must first be known by him. St. Paul was stating this truth when he said, "Now I know in part; then I shall understand fully, even as I have been fully understood" (1 Cor. 13:12). Or Jeremiah has God speaking to him, "Before I formed you in the womb I knew you" (Jer. 1:4). The clearest example of God's knowing us is in the great 139th Psalm:

O Lord thou hast searched me and known me!
Thou knowest when I sit down and when I rise up;
   thou discernest my thoughts from afar.

. . . .

Even before a word is on my tongue
   lo, O Lord, thou knowest it altogether.

. . . .

Such knowledge is too wonderful for me;

. . . .

Thou knowest me right well;
   My frame was not hidden from thee

. . . .

[19

Search me, O God, and know my heart!
    Try me and know my thoughts!
And see if there be any wicked way in me,
    and lead me in the way everlasting!

As one scholar has said, "not aspiration but receptivity is the movement of the Christian Gospel."[2]

And if knowing God is tied up with his knowing us and his revelation to us, then it should be clear that this biblical conception of knowledge is based upon love. This kind of knowledge even between human beings is not merely cognition; it depends upon love to ascertain it and as a consequence results in love.

When we give ourselves in love and trust, then we can have knowledge of another—on the deepest level. This can be seen in the relationship between two people. It can certainly be seen in our relationship to God. The result of both relationships is shared and mutual love. We can only know deeply as the one loved chooses to let us know.

In St. Paul's view, "only the man who loves God is 'known' by God. Being known by God is being saved by God's grace. This requires the Christian to learn to know himself as God knows him."[3]

"Knowledge" puffs up, but love builds up. If any one imagines that he knows something, he does not yet know as he ought to know. But if one loves God, one is known by him (1 Cor. 8:1-3).

But the glorious thing about this knowledge is that

it enables us to accept ourselves as we are and thus to be ourselves. This frees us for a more creative development on our own and certainly with other people. Paul discusses this kind of knowledge in Galatians 4:9.

> Formerly, when you did not know God, you were in bondage to beings that by nature are no gods; but now that you have come to know God, or rather to be known by God, how can you turn back again to the weak and beggarly elemental spirits, whose slaves you want to be once more?

Thus, the self-discovery brings responsibility although it gives freedom. The lines of George Matheson's hymn say it for us:

> Make me a captive, Lord, and then I shall be free;
> Force me to render up my sword, and I shall conqueror be.

This is the strange paradox of life that the man who is most bound to someone or something big enough to demand his loyalty is the most free. There are responsibilities in such a loving relationship, but there is also self-discovery.

I am sure you have all had the experience of being told about someone you should meet. Perhaps it is a prospective candidate for a fraternity or a sorority from your home town or perhaps a friend of the family whom you have never met. You know about the per-

son. You may even know all of his qualities and attri-
butes. Perhaps you even know some of his personality
traits. You know enough to make you believe that this
person is a reality. You know he exists and even more,
you have knowledge of him handed to you by others.
Then you are introduced to him and become ac-
quainted with him—you become casual friends. Perhaps he becomes a roommate and you live a year or
so with him. You enter then into a different relationship of experience and knowledge than you had before. As you share experiences and personalities, a
bond grows which transcends the previous superficial
knowledge you had. You begin to sense each other's
likes and dislikes, moods and tastes. You can really be
a friend of that person when you give yourself to the
relationship and participate wholly in it. Your fears
and apprehensions are lessened in that deep friendship. You become yourself. You are accepted. When
you do him wrong you are forgiven even before you
are asked. You feel obligation toward him, yet an obligation which is freely elicited and freely given.

So it is with self-identity and our relation to others.

III.

What then are the results of this self-identity, this
knowledge of ourselves?

In regard to the value of the relationship, we are

able to accept ourselves, know ourselves for what we are, and thereby we can destroy the false images of ourselves that we project instead of the real "me." Indeed, it is only as we know ourselves that we are enabled to become something different—more high, more noble. The psychiatrist who works with people who are trying to find the real "me" and then accept it may give us insight into ourselves and how we got that way. But only a high love that accepts us and redeems us can challenge us to new and higher behavior and deeper discovery.

In relation to others, I am enabled to enter into a deep relationship that is meaningful and real. Many of our relationships are not. Holden Caulfield in Salinger's fascinating novel, *The Catcher in the Rye*, illustrates this negatively. "He is a boy who is biased by the need for love, but what he generally finds in people is the slothful moral imagination, the underdeveloped heart, an incapacity for generousness, or unwillingness to be genuinely present to one another. And there seems to be no escape from his basic solitude."[4]

Self-identity permits us to escape from our human solitude and to have meaningful relationships with others. Frankie Adams, the twelve-year-old in *The Member of the Wedding*, feels this solitude disappear when she sees herself as part of her brother and his bride. She cries, "they are the *we* of me."[5] There is something in all of us which cries wistfully to be part of the *we* of someone else. We can love freely, for we have been loved and our defenses are down. As Browning puts it:

> Be love your light and trust your guide,
>   with these explore my heart!
> No obstacle to trip you then, strike hands
>   and souls apart![6]

We see this self-identity on the deepest human level, of course, in marriage. In many ways marriage is the opposite of romantic love as we commonly know it. In marriage you don't have to play the game. You are accepted for what you are. There is love and mutual trust. Obligations and responsibilities to be sure, but the joyous freedom of being known, discovered, and accepted for what you are.

Timmy was a ten-year-old boy in an orphanage. He was withdrawn, irascible, fearful, and sensitive. One day a childless couple came to the orphanage and took Timmy home with them. He had never known parents or a home and was puzzled by all this. At first he was rebellious and then questioning. But the "new" parents responded with only love and gifts. If he could have put his thoughts and feelings into words he might have said something like, "Why are they doing all this for me? They owe me nothing. I'm not biologically or legally tied to them." But after awhile Timmy's shell began to crumble and he responded gratefully to the love he had received. For the first time, Timmy had discovered his self-identity. He was no longer an unidentified object. He was a person, free to be himself because he had been accepted in love. True, he now had responsibilities he didn't have before; he was now bound with obligations in a way he had never been, but he accepted these gratefully knowing that he had been accepted and allowed to become his true self.

Here then is the secret of self-identity or self-discovery. When we give ourselves in faith to God for his loving us and for the gift of his Son, we are enabled to know ourselves and become ourselves.

"What's
in a Name?"

"What's in a Name?"

Exodus 3:1-15
Philippians 2:1-11

Some time ago I was reading everybody's favorite theologian—Peanuts! Charlie Brown is standing in line his first day at camp waiting for lunch. The fellow behind asks, "What's your name, kid?" "Charlie Brown," replies our hero. "Hey, everybody," says the fellow, "get a load of the kid with the funny name!" Charlie, embarrassed and dejected, can only say, "Lunch is gonna taste awful!"

This cartoon raises many interesting questions about names beyond their use as a signification of the individual. It shows the relation of the name to the personality; and it dramatizes the relationship between the emotional depths and the name. Although we smile at the comic strip, there's much more than humor involved in the importance and significance of names. For names reach to the depths of our very existence. Although a label may appear to be a merely external thing, it can reach to the marrow of our bones. The childhood doggerel

> Sticks and stones may break my bones,
> But names will never hurt me

is, of course, nonsense. Calling us names can murder us.

I.

The concern with names is not merely a recent problem. Shakespeare puts the words in Juliet's mouth,

> What's in a name? that which we call a rose
> By any other name would smell as sweet.[1]

Shakespeare was a great dramatist and poet, but a lousy semanticist. A rose by another name would not smell as sweet. Send some roses to your favorite gal and label them *rhubarb*. Then see if she sniffs them with the same relish. Or, let a local grocery label their hamburger *horse meat* and see how much they can move at 19¢ a pound. If there's anything we have learned from general semantics it is that words as names and labels reach right into our nervous system.

An innocent word can make us sick, or fearful, or excitable, or exhilarated.

In the pre-television days when Candid Camera was Candid Microphone, a man stood in front of Marshall Fields in Chicago keeping a lot of people out of the store by telling them that the building was "retroactive." We can smile at the ignorance of the people who were confused, but the incident shows the power of words in relation to the depths of our being.

Kazantzakis in *The Greek Passion*[2] tells the story of a village in Greece which during the Easter season every seven years played out the passion drama, the roles being assigned by the priest. Of course, the people's characters had something to do with the roles assigned, but the significant thing was that they became the characters they were to play. It was as if assigning them the name started a chemical change within them, and they automatically became the names assigned.

We do not need fiction to dramatize the fact of the power of names, however. Psychologists remind us of the relationship between name and being. A few years ago the *American Institute of Hypnosis Journal* reminded parents that they should choose their children's first names with care lest they cause them insurmountable psychological problems. Said the *Journal:* "A person's name is the most important sound in the world to him, and his response to it often causes trouble."[3] Criminality and maladjustment follow

[31

selection of ill-advised names. For example, Jesus, a frequent Latin American name, may often cause rebellion—the opposite of what the name suggests. A name with a confusing gender may confuse a boy as to his. An example is Caryl as in Caryl Chessman. And even Junior should be avoided, say the good doctors. The son immediately feels he should exceed his father's qualities be they good or bad. It is a "stress-provoking" name.

Names can conjure up all sorts of feelings—often depending upon our reactions to people who have had certain names and whether that reaction is favorable or unfavorable. I well remember the raised eyebrow we got when we named our little girl Molly, and the further horror when it was discovered that it was not a nickname. The relatives were relieved a bit to discover that we had put in a good, solid, old-fashioned Ann in the middle to bail her out when she got older and became ashamed of being Molly.

We are suggesting, then, that names, which we usually take for granted, are more than labels; they reach into our innermost being; they are somehow tied up with our very existence.

II.

Now this concern for names has been at the heart of the Hebrew-Christian tradition. The Bible is replete with the sacredness of names and their importance.

The call of Moses is an outstanding example. Moses, approached by the Divine through the burning bush experience, sought to have this Being identify himself. God tried to identify himself by claiming that he was the object of worship of Moses's ancestors. Even this is not enough for Moses. "When I say to my people in Egypt that the God of your fathers has sent me, this won't be enough for them. They will ask, 'What's his name?' " And God told him, "I am who I am. Say, 'I Am' sent you." This may have helped Moses, but it does not help us much. God persists. He tries to identify himself now as the Lord (standing for Yahweh), the God who is the God of their fathers, and he tells Moses that this is his name forever.

A recent Catholic version of the Bible has been published with the word "Yahweh" replacing the word "Lord," because Yahweh means "the incommunicable name of God. Yahweh was not intended as a proper name, but on the contrary, was meant to indicate in some way that God cannot be named."[4]

It is quite clear how important names are, beginning with God's. In fact, the first thing to be said about his name is that he is too sacred to name—at least lightly. God only needs a personal name when there are other gods. When there is one God, he is it. Hence, I AM. God is being itself, too awe-inspiring to name, but when he is finally named, it should be one that exhausts the possibilities of that name, God. The third commandment which refers to taking God's name in vain makes more sense in this connection than in preventing us from swearing. Taking God's name in vain means putting his name on the wrong things. It is perjuring his name. It could easily belong to the other commandment of having no other gods before him—idolatry. The same might be said for the petition in the Lord's prayer. "Hallowed be thy name." He is really too sacred to name, but if we do, it should be with fear and trembling.

James Joyce, of all people, caught this in *A Portrait of the Artist As a Young Man*. He has the young boy Stephen thinking: "God was God's name just as his name was Stephen. *Dieu* was the French for God and that was God's name too; and when any one prayed to God and said *Dieu* then God knew at once that it was a French person that was praying. But though there were different names for God in all the different languages in the world and God understood what all the people who prayed said in their different languages, still God remained always the same God and God's real name was God."[5]

God's name also has power. Moses, speaking in God's *name*, had power, could perform miracles, and truly lead his people, because of the power of God's *name* used as his accreditation. Indeed, in the Bible, "the name of God is used frequently as a synonym for God himself."[6] J. D. Salinger caught something of this as Franny talks about the "Jesus prayer" used in India by mystics who repeat the Divine name—almost mechanically—but they become spiritual and learn to pray incessantly. Says she, "Any name of God—any name at all—has this peculiar, self-active power of its own, and it starts working after you've sort of started it up." She goes on ". . . if you repeat the name of God incessantly, something happens."[7]

In the Bible, not only is God's name sacred and powerful, but man's name is important too. A man's name is the essence of his personality, the expression of his innermost being. It is not a mere label of identification, but is rather an expression of the essential quality of its bearer. A man's name reveals his character; it does not merely distinguish him from other persons.

The name—as in the case of God—denotes essential being. Name is bound up with existence. Nothing exists unless it has a name. The act of creation was not complete until all creatures received a name. God's gift to Adam of naming the living things was a great gift. A kind of immortality is the name perpetuated by a man's descendants. To cut off a name is to end the existence of its bearer.

The name is so important to a man's personality in the Bible that a change of personality automatically means a change of name. In the 32nd chapter of Genesis we have depicted the story of Jacob's all-night wrestling match. When it was over, Jacob's name was changed to Israel, for he had striven with God and men and had prevailed. Know a man's name and you had a way open to the secret of the person. In the New Testament, Saul of Tarsus became Paul when he entered into the new life of a Christian. So it is that biblical religion records that the naming of a child is connected in some way to his personality. Choosing a child's name is of great importance.

To know the name of someone also involves a relationship with that person, and the responsibility of being known. That is, to know the name of God is to know God as he is revealed, or as he reveals himself. To be called by God's name is to be his possession and therefore to come under both his authority and his protection. The name of God means primarily his revealed nature and character—the Savior God as he has manifested himself and desires to be known.

For the Christian, of course, the name and the revelation of God culminate in Jesus Christ. To believe in the name of Christ—the name which is above every name—signifies that Christ is worthy of trust and that he can perform what his name implies. The full disclosure of God's nature and character is given in Jesus Christ, who manifested God's name. And to be baptized in Christ's name (in the name of Christ) means that we are his property, that we belong to him. The name of Jesus is in a sense a synonym for Jesus himself. It epitomizes his personality. Believing in the name of Jesus involves our acceptance of Jesus himself as Messiah and the obligation to show forth his love.

III.

When we come to the relevance of all this to you and me we should already be aware of some things. For one thing, we should take names seriously. I am sure one of the punishments for prisoners is to take away their names and give them numbers. Without a name a man loses his identity—a portion of his existence.

Our name may be tied inextricably to our identity and our vocation. Earlier we mentioned James Joyce's *A Portrait of the Artist as a Young Man.* One writer speaking of the hero says, "The importance to Stephen of names, particularly of his own name, is tremendous, because a name is to him not simply a sound or an utterance to attract the attention of its bearer. A person is his name, and he has to discover the meaning of his name in order to discover the meaning of himself. For Stephen to tell Nasty Roche that he did not know what kind of name Stephen Dedalus was, was to tell Nasty that he did not know himself. Joyce's novel traces Stephen's growing awareness of who he is and what he should be. In other words, it is a novel of vocation: what Stephen was called is the key to Stephen's calling."[8] Finding out who we are, why we are here, and where we are going is finding the meaning of our name.

Above all, names give us tremendous responsibility —whether they are our own or those we assume. And we do choose some names for ourselves, although we may not be quite like the character Starbuck in the play the *Rainmaker*. He is a con artist who stops at the Curry farm in the drought-stricken midwest and intrigues Lizzie the unmarried daughter. She knows he is a phony, yet he charms her. She accuses him of making up his name and he says,

> "Why not? You know what name I was born with? Smith! Smith, for the love of Mike. *Smith.* Now what kind of a handle is that for a fellow like me? I needed a name that had the whole sky in it! And the power of a man! Starbuck! Now there's a name—and it's mine."
> "No, it's not. You were born Smith—and that's your name."
> "You're wrong, Lizzie. The name you choose for yourself is more your own than the name you were born with."[9]

We were all given some name, but we also choose some important names in life which may be as important as our own, and they leave indelible prints. For example, most of us are associated one way or another with the Christian church. We cannot wear that label casually. We, individually, are an extension of the church. It is part of us and we of it. Even when we are distressed about our church, its recalcitrant laymen, its ineffective ministers, its stands on issues or lack of them, we are still part of it, even when we criticize loudly.

And above all, we wear the name *Christian*. The biblical view is that the name possesses an inherent power which exercises a constraint upon its bearer; he must conform to his essential nature as expressed in his name. We who are baptized Christians are not exactly our own any more—for we have been bought by a price. God risked a lot in coming to man, but we carry now a lot of responsibility because he did. We have been baptized into Christ. We are his church— the extension of his incarnation. Our attitudes in personal relations, in social situations, in our political and social concerns can never be the same again. We cannot even express our own personal preferences, our family's views, or even our peer groups' views alone. The name Christian takes precedence over all other loyalties and all other names. We go out every day named Christians—the most authentic and real name we have. We must never carry this name *Christian* lightly.

Remember again the play *The Rainmaker*. Lizzie and Starbuck continue their conversation. Starbuck tries to tell her that Lizzie isn't much of a name and she should change it to Leonora or Melisande. And he makes up a story to impress her about King Hamlet getting Melisande the Golden Fleece. Lizzie accuses him of lying, but he says he was dreaming. Lizzie replies that there are quiet dreams not fancies, based upon reality. "Like a man's voice saying, 'Lizzie is my blue suit pressed?' And the same man saying,

'Scratch between my shoulder blades.' And kids laughing and teasing and setting up a racket. And how it feels to say the word 'Husband.' There are all kinds of dreams, Mr. Starbuck. Mine are small ones—like my name—Lizzie. But they're *real* like my name —real."[10]

Our life-long quest will be the attempt, with God's help, to live up to the *reality* of our name CHRISTIAN.

Anyone
for Shepherding?

Anyone for Shepherding?

Ezekiel 34:11-16; 30-31
1 Peter 2:19-25

Jackie Vernon, one of our modern deadpan and sardonic comedians, often opens his act by stating: "I am just doing this because I can't find a job in my regular profession. I'm a shepherd." One of the reasons he tends to get laughs with this line is that shepherds and sheep mean very little to us in our urban civilization. A shepherd *is* a strange profession for most of us.

One of the reasons the Bible remains so strange to moderns is the pastoral analogies. We think in different categories from the biblical writers. Even though our church plays often have people with bathrobes on and towels on their heads, we never seem to be able to transfer them or their ideas into modern dress.

In speaking to ministers about shepherds (we often refer to ministers as *shepherds* or *pastors*), I have occasionally suggested that down in Marlboro country the figure of the cattle rustler might be more realistic. Many preachers in building their herds jump neighbors' fences, lasso strays, and put their own brands on them.

But, regardless of the shepherd figure, most of us don't like to think of ourselves as sheep. Oh, occasionally in a romantic moment some boy on a campus might call his girl "lambie-pie" or "lambkins" but he probably would not trumpet it from the top of the administration building. But when the Bible refers to us as sheep, it does not mean much to us, or we do not understand it, and we certainly do not care much for the compliment—if that is what it is meant to be!

I.

Unfortunately, most of us cannot escape the label— even in the derisive sense. If we think of sheep as dumb, unaggressive, defenseless, easily led, many people today feel that this pretty well describes those of us who live in university and college settings. That is, in spite of Berkeley, there is a lot of criticism that most of us are pretty sheeplike. We are interested more in *conformity* than *causes*. One of the often-heard criticisms of those of us who are members of fraternities is that we are sheeplike; we conform, we herd together, we are easily led. We do things in the group that we would not think of doing as individuals —at least outsiders tell us this with a certain element of truth. But not only the Greeks: the whole collegiate community of our day has this problem. We *do* conform; we *are* easily led; we follow fads. We seek conformity in dress and style. The skirts go up and down together for the girls; the boys cut their hair— or not—together. But fad-following is not serious. This is only symptomatic of our deeper problems of sheeplike behavior—*conformity*. We are told that we are materialistic; we tend to play it safe. We think alike; vote alike; have similar desires; we want the same things: security, success, materialism, wealth.

In *Newsweek,* James A. Wechsler called the present generation a group of "flaming moderates." In a series of interviews asking college students what they wanted to be doing fifteen years from now, the answers were:

"I'll be secure financially."

". . . will be somewhat similar to my parents, upper middle class, etc."

". . . mother of five boys. Live in Pennsylvania. Live in modern circular home that is completely automatic."

". . . will be working and living in a $35,000 home overlooking a mortgage."[1]

[45

What *do* we see when we close our eyes and look into the future? The picture can be drawn for most of us: there is a ranch-style, three bedroom and den, air-conditioned home, a sports car in the driveway alongside a country squire wagon, a boat on a trailer, skis stowed overhead in the garage, the hero in bermuda shorts, a white knit sports shirt with an alligator on the pocket, the heroine in capri pants, steaks on the grill and a frozen daiquiri in each hand. Is that our dream?

Unfortunately, such a picture is not overdrawn. One day I talked with a senior girl who had been idealistic all her college career, interested in many worthwhile causes, stepping out and taking a stand for unpopular but exciting movements. Finally, I noticed she had quit this kind of activity and was pinned to a rather unimaginative and short-sighted young man who was going to sell bonds. When I asked her about this, she replied, "Well, after all, I have the future to think of." Yes, we do conform. Yes, there is a sense in which we are sheep, and even though we do not like it, in all honesty we must admit that it is so.

II.

When we turn to the biblical faith we still find that we are sheep, but there is one important difference. In the Bible there is always the relationship between

the sheep and the shepherd. This relationship is of
strategic importance. The Old Testament lesson from
Ezekiel shows God judging bad shepherds. They feed
themselves instead of the sheep. They have not
strengthened the weak or healed the sick. They have
not gone out to look for the lost and have treated the
sheep with harshness. Thus, the sheep are scattered.
Ezekiel, of course, is talking about Israel and her
rulers, but the teaching is universal. God will rescue
the sheep from false shepherds. *He* himself will gather
the sheep and feed them. *He* will be the Shepherd.
He will seek the lost, bring back the strayed, and
bind up the crippled. *He* will strengthen the weak
and watch over the strong and feed them all in justice.
In other words, there is judgment against false shepherds; God is the true Shepherd. *He* will judge the
sheep and will give them a true shepherd—David
—to act for him. The basic insight here is that God
claims the sheep. *"You are my sheep."*

> Know that the Lord is God!
> It is he that made us, and we are his;
> we are his people, and the sheep of his pasture

says the psalmist (Ps. 100:3).
Now what is the response of sheep to such a claim
as this? We catch a glimpse of the response in the 23rd
Psalm:

> The Lord is my shepherd, I shall not want;

He makes me lie down in green pastures.
He leads me beside still waters;
    he restores my soul.
He leads me in paths of righteousness
    for his name's sake.

The New Testament enlarges the concept of the Shepherd and the sheep chiefly through the differing role of the Shepherd. Isaiah hinted at this new Shepherd concept (53:6-7).

All we like sheep have gone astray;
    we have turned every one to his own way;
and the Lord has laid on him
    the iniquity of us all.
He was oppressed, and he was afflicted,
    yet, he opened not his mouth;
like a lamb that is led to the slaughter,
    and like a sheep that before its
        shearer is dumb,
    so he opened not his mouth.

For the Christian, Jesus has become the Good Shepherd. He knows his own, "and he had compassion on them, because they were like sheep without a shepherd (Mark 6:34). He loves them, is concerned about all sheep, and above all lays down his life for the sheep. See what a new dimension this is! Not an animal sacrifice—as a lamb perhaps—but the Shepherd himself who gives his life for the sheep. The shepherd dying for his sheep.

The first epistle of Peter gives us still another dimension. Here the faithful Christians have seen the example of the Good Shepherd. They are under persecution and are suffering in his Name. They are urged to suffer patiently, remembering his example who suffered in their name. They had formerly strayed like sheep, but are now his. They are reminded to live as his servants; patient and in love, enduring the suffering.

Now we see the motifs of biblical faith and the Christian gospel. First, the sheep belong to God. God himself claims the sheep. Second, Jesus himself becomes the Good Shepherd who knows and loves the sheep—even giving his life for them. Third, the sheep are to live in love and faithfulness, even though they may have to endure suffering—even perhaps a cross itself.

III.

When we return from the biblical view to the *now*, we begin to see ourselves in different perspectives. We are still sheep. Even if we do not like the image, sheep we are. Our problem is not in being sheep, but in not having the right shepherd. This has a twofold implication. First, it upsets my temptation to be my own shepherd, to see myself as the master of my fate and the captain of my soul, to see myself as the center of my universe with my goals, ambitions, dreams my focal point. It reminds me that I am not my own, for I have been bought with a price. It also says to me that other sheep or small-caliber shepherds are not big enough for me to trust my destiny to. Materialism, conformity, political parties, national policy, social and racial prejudices—none of these is worthy of ultimate allegiance if we know we have been claimed by the Good Shepherd.

I am further reminded that the sacrifice the Good Shepherd made still occurs in our day in his Name. Living in our day still involves crucifixion for the right. Earlier we mentioned how Kazantzakis in *The Greek Passion* tells the fascinating story of a village in Greece which reenacts the Passion Week. The characters of the pageant are selected and strangely enough they become the parts they are assigned: Peter, Judas, Mary Magdalene, Christ. The latter is a simple shepherd boy Manolios. Throughout the book, we see his becoming the figure he is selected to portray. Survivors of a gutted village come by seeking asylum but are refused by the town fathers, and they go on to live in the rocky crags beyond the town. As Manolios attempts to respond to these people's needs, he is turned upon by his own townspeople, is scourged and finally killed. Yes, there is still the sacrificial nature of life for those who live Christianly—who remember an earlier sacrifice. This does not mean going off like an erratic Don Quixote to fight runaway windmills. There is a cruciform pattern to life, and for the

one who leads it there will be sacrifice aplenty—
especially if we live our lives in Christ's Spirit.

This faith then does not mean a pious faith which
expresses itself in sentiment, but does nothing actively.
Manolios the shepherd tells of a visit to him by Christ.
The Master says:

"Why do you stay here, you who say you love me,
why do you stay here, nice and quiet and with your
arms folded, resting? You eat, you drink, you read
at your ease the words which I have spoken, you
weep at the story of my crucifixion, and then you
go to bed and sleep. Aren't you ashamed? Is that
how you love me? Do you call that love? Get up!"[2]

Our love and feelings for others, possibly even suffering, are more than vicariously deciding to give
something monetary for a relief fund—a guilt offering.

I listen to the agony of God
I who am well fed
Who never yet went hungry for a day
I see the dead
The children starved for lack of bread
I see and try to pray.

I listen to the agony of God
But know full well
That not until I *share* their bitter cry
Earth's pain and hell
Can God within my spirit dwell
To bring His Kingdom nigh.[3]

[51

Now I don't know what this might mean for you. Each one must decide for himself, but decide he must —yes or no. For one it might mean a year in the Peace Corps instead of that comfortable fellowship in graduate school; it might mean for another teaching in the headstart program; for another it might mean working in some social service program. For all of us, it should mean something more active in the fields of human rights and social justice, of witnessing against war as the only solution to human problems, of refusing to be a part of the degradation of any individual, of standing for what we believe in spite of crowd pressure, of sticking to our guns in regard to moral rightness no matter what the Gallup poll of any particular norm might be.

These are the things which are our mandate for being sheep—but special kind of sheep. Sheep who belong to the right Shepherd who sacrificed himself for us and calls upon us to love and serve in his Name.

In his novel *The Lamb*, François Mauriac tells the story of a young student who is on his way to school but on a train becomes involved with a man and his family problems. Out of compulsion he goes home with the stranger and enters his household. Thereupon Xavier becomes involved in the tortured, torn, and twisted lives of the Mirbel family. As he tries to reconcile these twisted individuals, he himself is enmeshed in their tragedies, and finally—irony of irony —he is sacrificially killed as he attempts to effect reconciliation. A few weeks later, the husband speaking to the wife as they attempt to pick up the pieces, says,

"Yes, Michele, I know now that *love* does exist in this world. But it is crucified in the world and we with it."[4]

Tragedy
and Triumph

Tragedy and Triumph

Luke 19:28-38; 23:33-35; 24:1-9

Writing of the American theater-going public, one critic says that "our audiences want to be harrowed (and even slightly shocked) from eight till ten-thirty, and then reassured before eleven." "Yes," says another, "what the American public wants *is a tragedy with a happy ending.*"[1] Although these comments may reflect our play-going tastes, it is debatable whether they reflect the mood of our society as a whole. Rather, a good case could be made that most of us revel in one extreme or the other—*tragedy* or *happiness* as a way of life.

I.

There are many people today who are satisfied with the tragedy of life. Unamuno, the Spanish philosopher, writes of the *Tragic Sense of Life,* and this seems to be the mood for many in our world. A few years ago a group of disenchanted T.V. writers led by the creative Paddy Chayefsky were discussing why they were leaving T.V. for the theater and the movies. One said:

> The most exciting work that I see is being done by writers who look around and see total disaster. And it may very well be that they're right. It may be that we are living in a culture that is headed for total disaster.[2]

Indeed, total disaster has become the theme for many of our writers. In Arthur Miller's *Death of a Salesman* we see a microcosm of the kind of tragedy which walks our streets. There are Willy Lomans in our midst who, if not taking the way of suicide, still live in the despair of meaninglessness. And in Theodore Dreiser's naturalistic novel *An American Tragedy* we see portrayed the tragedy of a young man enmeshed in inevitable forces over which he has no control.

But this is not alone the philosophy of our writers. Many ordinary people feel the same way. The person who visits Europe and gets behind the newspapers and the hot words of the cold war is often impressed by the meaninglessness and despair expressed by the ordinary person he meets. The German, for instance, who has experienced the ravages of war sees the East-West struggle as only a game, and plods along unmoved by the flutterings of the doves of peace; he waits only for the inevitable day when he is enveloped in the last great holocaust.

But the despair and tragedy to be seen in the world is not only that of man facing titantic forces over which he has no control. Some of the tragedy is of a sophisticated nature buttressed by an intellectual philosophy. From the times of the Greeks with scepticism, cynicism, and stoicism on down through Nietzsche and Jean Paul Sartre we see tragedy given a rationale. The modern existentialist who sees no hope beyond the moment of his existence has given a sophisticated respectability to the tragedy which the ordinary man feels in his bones.

But it is not only the ordinary man, the existentialists, and the writers who signify and give expression to the modern tragic sense of life. Tragedy has been baptized into the church and many Christians even have grounded their faith in a kind of stoic hopelessness. This view, conditioned more often by sociological than theological factors, enables our faith to rise no higher than our present situation with perhaps a nod to an ultimate, faraway victory by a God who is content, deist-like to fly above the storm.

[59

The ethics of tragedy, whether Christian or not, can bog down into a moment-by-moment relativity shattering whatever absolutes one pleases. Monogamy is a mockery; sex is a tool to be used for the gratification of the moment; self-concern is primary, exemplifying itself in Sartre's dictum that "Hell is other people."[3]

Now this is not to say that life is not tragic in many of its aspects. We do live in a world of tragedy. Today only a schizophrenic Nero enjoys playing the fiddle while the Romes of the world burn.

II.

But to recognize the all-pervading aspects of the tragic does not complete the picture. For, on the other hand, and at the other extreme, the pessimists have a valiant opponent in optimism. It is interesting to note that in a time such as ours some react to events by succumbing to them while others tend to ignore them.

On the most elementary level we can see this optimism, romanticism, and happiness cult in our living rooms on T.V. With Bonanza, High Chaparral, and Gunsmoke, we can all be involved in riding a stagecoach of escape into the West where we can see evil blasted by the two guns of righteousness slung low on the hips of our heroes: that is, ourselves in projection. The simplicity of right and wrong makes the choice easy—in fantasy. Shirley Temple used to help us by assuring us that the heroine gets rescued and the villain will at least be dressed in black so the moral will be crystal clear. Or we can recall, as one writer points out, that the Robert Montgomery show was interested only in "happy shows for happy people." And there is always that positivist, Lawrence Welk, who can help us dance into the champagne bubbles of buoyancy whenever we feel that life gets too tough.

But this view has its antecedents too. From the time of the Epicureans right down through the German Idealists in philosophy, the Romantics in literature, to some modern Madison Avenue executives, the happiness cult is established. Now this optimistic view of things, which has a high regard for man's goodness and at the same time a penchant for overlooking tragedy, is not alone the province of idealistic philosophy or romantic literature. It, too, has found its way into religion through various forms of mysticism, peace of mind cults, irrelevant biblicisms, and humanisms which enable us to think and act positively in the face of evil.

The problem, of course, with an optimistic view of life which does not include or which tries to overlook evil is that it may itself end up in tragedy.

A good friend of mine told me recently that he no longer got much from Browning. When he said this I was shocked, for Browning had been his hero. "No," he said, "the optimism of Browning does not fit life as I now know it." No longer could he sing, "God's in his heaven—All's right with the world!" Nor could he say with Rabbi Ben Ezra, "Welcome each rebuff That turns earth's smoothness rough." Or, "Grow old along with me! The best is yet to be." This man had recently been dealt a tragic blow in the loss of loved ones and was now facing the last few years in chronic loneliness. What has Browning to say to him?

Yes, the problem with the optimistic view of life is that it tries to escape from tragedy by oversimplifying on the one hand, or on the other by trying to maintain itself as a way of life and ending in tragedy itself. Even the Western heroes are not all good and bad, morally speaking. They seem complicated and hard to simplify. Even "Robert Montgomery Presents" has left the air. When the optimistic bubble bursts— and burst it will if not tempered with the realism of the tragic—then despair and tragedy result. In a real sense, then, both the optimistic and the tragic views of life eventually reach the same level of despair, hopelessness, and meaninglessness.

III.

But it is at this precise point that the Christian gospel comes to bear. From the Bible right down through history to Kierkegaard, Dostoevsky, and Paul Tillich there is the unrelenting theme that in the midst of despair and meaninglessness the condition for faith is ripe. Out of the ruins of our own self-concerns, the Christian gospel will have meaning for each one of us.

And this brings us back to our opening quotation about the drama critic's appraisal of American tastes. "We want a tragedy with a happy ending." Well, there is a sense in which all men on the deepest level, while not necessarily desiring tragedy, but recognizing tragedy in life, desire a victory over it. Not a superficial happiness which comes on the stage at 10:40, but an assurance that the author of the cosmic drama knows how the story will turn out, is concerned with the actors, and will resolve the play in an ultimate victory. This is the happy or victorious ending for which all men cry wistfully.

The Christian faith speaks to our time as no other way of life can, for it deals realistically with our woes. It does not overlook the evils and tragedies of life— nor does it wallow in the tragic muck without a saving word. No, if there is any meaning to the Incarnation it is certainly at the point of affirming that "God was in Christ reconciling the *world* [with all its tragedies and triumphs] to himself" (1 Cor. 5:19).

It is at this point that the Scripture comes to bear. It is no accident that the basis for this sermon has been not only the Palm Sunday passages, but the Crucifixion and Resurrection passages as well. To see Palm Sunday without Good Friday is a shallow optimism. This is exactly what many of Jesus' followers did. When they saw Jesus' arrival as a triumphant entry, they were exultant. When they believed he would set up an earthly kingdom and overthrow the Roman government, they were buoyant. Even those closest to Jesus were filled with hopes which they expected to be fulfilled within the week. But Good Friday ruined the shallowness of Palm Sunday for many disciples, and hence they became disaffected, disappeared, even denied their Lord. There is not much triumph in singing:

> Ride on! ride on in majesty!
> In lowly pomp ride on to die![4]

Stopping with only Palm Sunday is a soured triumph turned to tragedy.

> The kingdoms of the world go by
> In purple and in gold;
> They rise, they flourish, and they die
> And all their tale is told.
>
> One kingdom only is Divine.
> One banner triumphs still,
> Its King a Servant, and its sign
> A gibbet on a hill.[5]

The Cross of Friday displaced the crowds of Palm Sunday.

On the other hand, Good Friday cannot be seen

apart from Easter morning. Of all the tragedies, the greatest would be that God's will was defeated at Calvary. We would indeed have reason for irredeemable hopelessness. "If Christ has not been raised, then our preaching is in vain and your faith is in vain" (1 Cor. 15:14). But that is not the Christian faith. The Christian faith is: "But thanks be to God, who gives us the victory through our Lord Jesus Christ" (1 Cor. 15:57). Jesus is not a dead martyr but the resurrected Son of God. This is the faith of the Christian church, a faith which does not ignore the tragedies of the world but looks at them realistically and tries to redeem them, knowing that God's ultimate victory cannot be denied.

IV.

Now what does all this have to say to you and me?

First of all, I suppose we can remember that the rhythm of tragedy and triumph is a continual motif in day-by-day living. The tragedies of life have their triumphs when seen and handled by people of faith. Most of us don't think much about tragedy. We are aware of the tragedy of huge hydrogen forces, but too often personal tragedies of life are so remote that we forget their existence. But they are all around us.

What about the student who discovers that after years of planning for a medical career he is not scholastically equipped to do the job? Or what about the coed who finds her engagement broken in May of her senior year before her September wedding? Or, the discovery of a lingering illness? Yes, even on the most personal levels we may find tragedies which leave us either in hopeless despair or which may be redeemed into triumphs. The boy who stumbled in organic chemistry in the pre-med course may discover that all of these years he was trying to please parents when his real desire was to be a high school teacher. The girl who found the summer an unbelievable period of hopelessness pulled herself together for another year of study in her major field. The illness may teach patience, consideration, and self-discovery.

We can admire courage like that—and for many of us these responses are just sheer courage. True, and yet the person of faith sees these not as examples of self-discipline, but as testimonies of faithfulness—of making our second choices victories.

Another lesson we can learn is that when anyone tries to exemplify Christian love in the world he may encounter tragedy. The person with genuine concern for others may have his motives suspect; the one who speaks of brotherhood may be called "pink"; the one who has an ethical standard may be proclaimed a "square." Yes, there is a price to pay, but remembering the Cross, the faithful Christian can pay that price. However, for the Christian there is not only a crucifixion, there is a resurrection as well.

Finally, there is the decisive victory of Christ over

death. This is the sign of God's great victory over the greatest tragedy and no Christian is able to lose sight of that.

In the preface to one of his volumes of the war years, Winston Churchill writes: "I have called this Volume *Triumph and Tragedy* because the overwhelming victory of the Grand Alliance has failed so far to bring general peace to our anxious world."[6] The Christian can say, "I have called this gospel *tragedy* and *triumph*, because the seeming victory of man's grand alliance of sin, disillusionment, and meaninglessness has been overcome in God's decisive victory in Christ." This is the gospel message; this is the tragedy with a victorious ending!

Two Minutes
Till Midnight

Two Minutes Till Midnight

Luke 12:13-34

The late Elmer Davis once wrote a book entitled *Two Minutes Till Midnight*. The title came from the cover of the *Bulletin of the Atomic Scientists* which had a clock with the hands at two minutes till twelve. At one time these hands were at eight to twelve, but this was before the Russians had the atomic bomb. The hands then moved to three minutes of twelve. When the Russians got the hydrogen bomb, the hands moved to two minutes till twelve; and now with even the Chinese getting into the hydrogen bomb race, these hands may even be closer.

Although Mr. Davis pointed out America's precipitous position, we need no one to tell us that we live under the sword of Damocles. Even though we don't like to think about it, any morning the headlines from South Vietnam, Cambodia, Laos or Thailand, Cuba or Berlin, remind us of the thin thread which supports and separates two hydrogen-bomb-loaded powers facing each other from different parts of the world.

There is a real sense then in which we live on the edge of eternity. In this kind of atmosphere, what we do with our lives seems of tremendous importance every moment of the day. The Scripture lesson, strangely enough, ties in a sense of urgency in life with a view of what's important. In other words, there's a sense of urgency about deciding what a person is after in life. In this motif, the Scripture has a ring of contemporaneity.

I.

First of all, the Scripture tells the story of a man who asked Jesus to divide his inheritance with his brother. Jesus dodged the question by reminding the man that he was not an umpire. But characteristically he put his finger on the problem by showing that the man didn't need an arbiter. His problem was greed—covetousness. Jesus remarked that " 'a man's life does not consist in the abundance of his possessions.' " Or as the *New English Bible* has it, " 'for even when a man has more than enough, his wealth does not give him life.' "[1] Or as Goodspeed translates the passage, " 'A man's life does not belong to him, no matter how rich he is.' "[2]

Now this clearly would not make a very good text for a baccalaureate sermon. If there is one thing in the world we are concerned about it is possessions. Of course, we all have our idealistic moments, but most of us are concerned first with material things—and then perhaps with idealism. This text turns upside down our standards, for we *do* think that life consists in what we possess. That's how the world measures success. Any science major or engineer knows what an exhilarating experience an interview with a large company can be. Salary, retirement benefits, incentive bonuses, vacation with pay—all are designed to help us buy status and possessions to fit our grandest dreams.

A few years ago on the now defunct Bob Newhart show there was a satirical sketch depicting company agents disguised as Good Humor Men and policemen descending on grade school playgrounds all over America signing up sixth graders for their firms. If we think that is overdrawn, I noticed in my wife's tenth year reunion book from Wellesley that 72 percent of the girls married men who in a short ten-year span were making up to $60,000. Yes, possessions are important to us, and we have the statistics to prove it.

But the gospel has a way of turning our standards upside down. Jesus' words about possessions are not exactly about possessions—they are about life. *Life* does not consist in the abundance of possessions. A man's wealth does not give him *life*. A man's *life* does not belong to him no matter how rich he is. In our most perspicacious moments, even the most crass among us are suspicious of our materialistic goals. We know—when we are being honest with ourselves —that ultimately we do not possess things; they possess us. I know men who should slow down their pace, but they have such a load of insurance premiums to keep up they cannot. I have friends who cannot take a vacation because they are afraid the weeds will take over their yards. Things have a way of taking over our lives when they become too important to us. It is easy to say that there are no Brink's armored cars in a funeral procession, but many of us feel that that must be a possibility. And yet—do we? Are we not really suspicious of the emphasis upon things?

Later on in this particular chapter, Jesus warns his listeners that where their treasure is, there will be their heart. In our deepest moments, we know that a heart of gold is a cold and merciless organ. The Master pointed out that the worldly seek treasures in things which thieves steal and moths destroy. He might have added that inflation, a failing bank, or the stock market can do the same thing. "A man's life does not consist in the abundance of his possessions."

II.

Secondly, Jesus was interested not only in a man's possessions. He was equally concerned about a person's *life*—how a man deals with himself. He tells his disciples, "Therefore, I tell you, do not be anxious about your life, what you shall eat, nor about your body, what you shall put on. . . . Consider the lilies, . . . they neither toil nor spin; yet I tell you, even Solomon in all his glory was not arrayed like one of these." He reminds them that the birds neither sow nor reap and yet they are fed. We are apt to say to this admonition, "That's for the birds!"

What are we to make of such a teaching? Does this mean an absolute prohibition of any forethought or providence on our part? Perhaps Jesus is using an Oriental figure of speech—an exaggeration. Maybe it is for the close followers only—disciples then and clergy now. Or as Albert Schweitzer and others have pointed out, perhaps these teachings are part of the interim ethic. Jesus was expecting the world to end soon, and thus it was necessary to "let goods and kindred go" to prepare to meet the judgment.

Yet all of these reactions may be our rationalizations. Perhaps this word is God's actual demand upon us in all times and for all time. As in the case with possessions, the problem is not the clothes and the food. All have need of them, but it is the *anxiety* about them—the furious pace to acquire which disintegrates our selfhood.

It would be foolish to emphasize our anxiousness. Hasn't ours been called "The Age of Anxiety"? On the national level, our military preparedness becomes a kind of frantic anxiety. Mao Tse-tung's digestion can

[75

send the stock market up and down. And on the personal level we know that lesser anxieties than food or clothes can give us ulcers or send us to a psychiatrist's couch.

This Scripture and the gospel simply remind us that worry is pagan. We are to be aware of God's providence—his loving care and concern—and live faithfully in response to that concern. We are to live off our faith, not off our anxieties. "O men of little faith! You are troubled about many things—one thing is needful."

III.

In the third place, Jesus moves from possessions and a man's concern for his life to his ultimate *goal.* He sums up the one thing needful: Instead of spending our energies worrying over the inconsequential in life, we are to "seek his kingdom, and these things shall be yours as well" (Luke 12:31). Note the emphasis. Not that goods are not important, but they need perspective. Another version says, "Set your heart on his kingdom, and your food and drink will come as a matter of course" (Phillips).[3] Why is it that the gospel constantly needs to remind us of what we suspect in our honest and solitary moments? Ultimately there is only one center of our lives that is worth building a life on—faith in God and his kingdom.

The Book of Isaiah gives us a wonderful picture of a modern pagan. In the 44th chapter, we are shown how a man makes his gods. First, he takes a tree, cuts it down, uses part of the wood to build a fire and warm himself; then he uses more to bake his bread; and then with the residue he makes a god to worship. See what the New Testament does to that image! It turns it upside down. First, says Jesus, seek God's kingdom, then be anxious about warmth (clothing), and then what to eat or drink. God's ways are not the ways of the world.

It would take a whole sermon to describe God's kingdom, but essentially it means for us to seek his way and his will above all. We are to live faithfully, following him in participating now in his kingdom which is already in the midst of us. It is finding the essential in life, focusing on it, making him the point North on our compass—then all these lesser things will be seen in perspective.

IV.

Now at last we come again to the note of urgency. Why is God's way in regard to life, possessions, and goals so important to us? Why did Jesus link them with urgency? Let's go back to the Scripture. In the midst of this passage Jesus told a story, as was his custom. A rich man had a bountiful crop and he said, "I have nowhere to store my crops." Then he decided to build bigger barns and to put all of his goods there. Then he thought: "Now I can take it easy. I can eat, drink, and be merry, and enjoy my *possessions*." Here was a man who had the farm surplus really working for him. But see what Jesus said: "Fool! This night your soul is required of you; and the things you have prepared, whose will they be?" Or, "You fool, this very night you must surrender your life; you have made your money—who will get it now?" It was two minutes till midnight for this first-century farm speculator. "Who will get it all now?" This night *your* soul may be required.

All of this says something to the nations of the world. As we face the cataclysm of war, it is two minutes till midnight. Can we handle our power, can we come to some agreement in the family of nations before the clock strikes? It is two minutes to midnight in regard to our relations with the uncommitted in the world, with the racial unrest in our society. Our time is short. It is two minutes till twelve.

And personally, too. Most of us are not concerned about our finiteness—our mortality. But we know we live on the brink of a hydrogen holocaust. We even know that our own lives may be demanded due to the uncertainties in life through disease, injury, accident, or death. It is two minutes till midnight as we go into the world to build a life.

In a sense, Calvary was two minutes to midnight, but to the faithful disciples there came the dawn of the Easter morn. It is only this kind of faith that can take us through the midnight hours of life.

Herman Hagedorn in the poem, "The Bomb That Fell on America" shows another way—a far better way—in which our souls can be demanded:

> "There is power in the human soul,"
>   said the Lord,
> "When you break through and set it free.
> Like the power of the atom.
> More powerful than the atom,
> It can control the atom,
> The only thing in the world that can.
> I told you that the atom is the greatest
>   force in the world, save one.
> That one is the human soul"[4]

This night our soul is required of all of us.

Albert Camus in his novel, *The Fall,* tells the story of Jean Clamence-Baptiste, a successful lawyer. He has an excellent practice, money, women, adulation— all the possessions an elegant Parisian could desire. But one night—perhaps two minutes till midnight?— as he was crossing the Seine, he heard laughter below the bridge which shocked him out of his self-righteous complacency. This laughter reminded him of another night some three years before when he had been crossing the bridge—the midnight hour?—and had heard the sound of a body striking the water. He stopped short, but did not respond to the cries for help. Then, he said, "Too late, too far . . ."[5] He had passed his moment of decision; his midnight hour; his respectable life was shattered.

It is two minutes till twelve! This night your life may be required of you and mine of me!

And the Walls
Came Tumbling Down

And the Walls Came Tumbling Down

Ephesians 2:11-22

Suppose we were to read in today's newspaper that the Berlin Wall was to come down! The two Germanies were to be reunited. Not, as now, an occasional pass over a special holiday, but free access all the time. And, further, the tearing down of the wall was simply a dramatic symbol for the fact that the two Germanies were being united again; there would no longer be hostility between East and West; the cold war was over.

Even with an occasional thawing of the icy atmosphere between East and West which we now experience from time to time, the reality of the above-reported news would take a vivid imagination.

I.

Yet, it is precisely the same kind of radical imagination that we need in order to picture what the writer of Ephesians is talking about. Here is a Jewish Christian writing to a group of Gentile Christians and recounting for them their history. He is telling them, first of all, that they were separated from Christ (v. 12). To make it even stronger, he reminds them they were alienated from the commonwealth of Israel. A man without a country would know this feeling, a person living on a foreign soil would know. And in our own country we see on television the reminders that all aliens living here must go to the nearest Post Office and register. These Gentiles had been aliens. They were strangers to the covenant; without hope and without God. They had had a dreary existence. They were both separated from Christ and separated from the first Christians—the Jewish converts.

The wall between the Gentiles and the Jews was almost insurmountable. The Berlin Wall suggests the size of the barrier. One searches for modern examples to dramatize the dreadful chasm between these two groups and what it would mean to bring them together. It would be similar to picturing the NAACP and the White Citizens Council having a picnic together in Selma, Alabama. Or, perhaps more realistically, it would be similar to the Jews and Arabs getting together in brotherly love and solving all of

84]

their problems over night. Even after the Jews became Christian, many still felt they were the chosen people. As Christians, they brought into the new church their food taboos and ritualistic ceremonies such as circumcision. They still tended to consider the Gentiles less than full Christians, not really part of the family. Gentile was a name given to outcasts; it was synonymous with being a pagan. A Gentile was a nothing.

Now it is this past history the author is reciting when he is reminding the Ephesians who they were when they were separated from Christ. They were separated, strangers, alienated, with no hope. What cold words! But, then, something happened!

II.

This wall of hostility was broken down (v. 14). *Through Christ Jesus,* he told them, *those of you who were far off were brought near. He brought peace, making us—Jew and Gentile—both one. In short, Jesus Christ has broken down the dividing wall of hostility.* Such picturesque language would be very meaningful to the Gentiles—as well as to the Jews. In the Temple at Jerusalem there was an inner court and an outer court. Only the Jews could enter the former and the visitors and outcasts had to stay in the outer court. A modern-day example would be the Mormon Temple in Salt Lake City. Those who have visited Temple Square know that visitors are not permitted in the Temple even though they can go into the Tabernacle. The Temple is reserved for extraordinary Mormons and actual Latter Day Saints.

The author of the Ephesian letter says this kind of separation cannot exist between people in the church. He pictures this inner court wall in the Jerusalem Temple destroyed, in the process removing that separation between the "good guys" and the "bad guys." With the Temple open, all would be granted entrance. He is telling the church at Ephesus that all these walls have been broken down through the Spirit of Christ. Christ has made one man out of two. No longer Jew and Gentile—only Christian. The hostility is ended.

III.

You have now become fellow citizens. No longer are you strangers or sojourners. You are fellow citizens with the saints (v. 19). Here the author is using a political analogy which would be perfectly clear to those living in the sphere of Roman influence. In essence he is saying that you late Christians are just as much citizens as the "native born"—in this case, the Jews. It was Will Rogers who once said, in speaking of his Indian blood as compared with that of the Daughters of the American Revolution, "My forefathers didn't come over on the *Mayflower*, but they met the boat." And this Jewish Christian is telling these Gentile Christians that they are no longer second-class citizens in the kingdom, but are first class in every way because of what Christ has done for them. How reminiscent this is of Jesus' parable of the late workers in the vineyard. The workers who came for the last hour were paid as much as those who came early in the day. The message is clear—those who come into the kingdom any time are accepted on the same basis as the first converts.

Then, as if to show his wide-ranging mind, the author changes his analogy to architecture. He tells the Ephesians that they are now members of the household of God whose foundation is the apostles and prophets. Jesus Christ is the cornerstone of this Temple which they, the Ephesians, are now part of as a dwelling place for God's Spirit (vv. 19-22). Here, then, is the new building of the church—no longer Jews versus Gentiles. The wall has come down. The church is both built into the household of faith.

IV.

When we look through the details and language of this ancient letter, we can see that we are reading a letter addressed to us. For are we not, as Christians, seeing here our personal history too? The perennial story of the church is that we are no longer aliens, strangers, or sojourners. We are members of the household of God and have fellowship with the saints. This change has been brought about by the life, teaching,

[87

death, and resurrection of Jesus Christ. And, because of him, the walls have come tumbling down.

These walls are everywhere—even within each of us. We have all heard of the man, described by Stephen Leacock, who got on a horse and rode off in all directions. That is the story of many of us, divided, warring against ourselves. How like the man in Mark 5 who was filled with so many spirits his name was Legion. How many of us cry with Paul, "The good that I would, I do not: but the evil which I would not, that I do" (Rom. 7:19. KJV)? But, Jesus did and does tame these divisive spirits, and tears down the walls that divide us. The walls of fear, frustration, anger, jealousy, and pettiness in each of us come down under Christ's influence.

Take the family. The walls between husbands and wives are dreadfully high these days. The number of mates who are merely playing roles in order to keep the family together is exceedingly high. Someone has said that most marriages have bogged down into a kind of tired friendship. Many pastors can have more knowledge of a person in twenty minutes than the person's mate has acquired in twenty years. Those are high walls in marriages. And, need we mention the walls between children and parents—the generation gap? We need something greater than ourselves to tear down these walls. Christ can and does do that for our families.

In other groups, too, Christ can bring down walls

that divide men—maybe he is the only one who can. No one is prophet enough to know what the future will be for the races, but we should know that laws alone will never be enough. But Christ's Spirit can bring them down. That Spirit needs to penetrate the church. One young man from Nigeria, converted by Methodist missionaries, discovered when he came to America to study that he could not worship in the very church that sent out the missionaries because of his color. A strange experience for a convert who might discover in the mission field a king worshiping side by side with a subject. We have come far in many respects, but there are still walls to be brought down —even in the church.

What about the relations with other Christians? There are centuries of high walls there, but they are coming down. Vatican II shows decisively that these walls of hostility built up over 500 years are coming down. When people ask if God is alive and working in the world today, then one needs only to point to the ecumenical movement of the churches. How can one doubt that Christ can bring walls down when we look at what is happening in the churches and in the relationships among Christians themselves.

What about the grass roots? Are these walls down in your community? The church should be a place where there are no walls. It should be filled with people who are wall breakers.

One of my closest Navy friends was in charge of

Ship's Service—the Navy stores—on an island in the Pacific. He tried to run the business as a civilian might run an efficient business at home. He had an ensign driving a truck, an ordinary seaman buying jewelry, a native islander civilian as the bookkeeper. One day the executive officer, a commander, came into the store and rebuked him for not running the store more like a military establishment. My friend remarked, "Commander, when anyone comes into this store, he hangs his rank on the door knob."

This true-life incident has always seemed to me to represent a modern parable for churchmen today. Just as the walls had to come down between the Jews and Gentiles in the Ephesian church, so our own desires, political persuasions, and pet peeves must stand aside in the church under the guidance of the Spirit of Christ. His Spirit destroys these walls that divide men and stands in judgment over all our own private dispositions which wall out others—and which wall out his Spirit. Further, we go from the church as disciples who are determined that our lives and witness will help to bring down the walls that separate men and groups in our society.

Robert Frost in "Mending Wall" says, "Something there is that doesn't love a wall."[1] Among other things, it is the Spirit of Christ.

The Last
Word

The Last Word

Job 38:1-18; 42:1-6
Matthew 27:41-54

Those of us who are married may not always know
what the last word is, but we can be reasonably sure
who is going to have it! To a husband, then, the last
word has a particular meaning. But there are other
areas too where there are last words: a midi skirt in
fashion. Or, in dramatic criticism, a theater critic may
be the last word. And at graduation time a lot of
platitudinous last words are offered seniors on com-
mencement programs all over America.

On the deepest level, I suppose we are all—in our
more somber moments—concerned to know what the
final, ultimate, and last word is going to be in our
personal destiny and above all, who is going to have
it.

I.

There are some pretty potent answers to these questions: What is the last word? Who will have it?

T. S. Eliot in *The Hollow Men* suggested that

> *This is the way the world ends*
> *This is the way the world ends*
> *This is the way the world ends*
> *Not with a bang but a whimper.*[1]

There are those in our day, realizing that Eliot wrote those lines in pre-Hiroshima days, who feel that it may end with a whimper to be sure, but also with a pretty sizable bang.

James Broughton in a play entitled, *The Last Word*,[2] tells of a couple who is awaiting a final hydrogen holocaust. They speak as follows:

Dusty: They've gotten the Word.
      Explosions begin in half an hour.
      It's in the papers. It's in the cards.
      The rapid transit has already ceased.
      That's the latest Word.
Rusty: What Word? Whose Word?
Dusty: How should one look? What should one wear?
Rusty: Is it the Last Word? Or the First Commandment?
      Is it the Second Coming?
      Or the Third Degree?

Dusty: I do hope it won't be messy.
Rusty: I hope it's a damn good show.

A little later the explosion does occur and the couple offers the following prayer:

Rusty: United Nations, have mercy upon us!
Dusty: Elizabeth Arden, deliver us!
Rusty: General Motors, have mercy upon us!
Dusty: Sigmund Freud, deliver us!
Rusty: Batten Barton Durstine and Osborne, have mercy upon us.
Dusty: In the name of Mutual Life and Cold Storage
Rusty: Amen.

Although the play is fiction, it is unfortunately true. There are those whose ultimate faith in our day seems to be in Elizabeth Arden, General Motors, Sigmund Freud, or Mutual Life. In fact, there is nothing fictitious in the struggle going on within our own government as to what and who will have the last word. Will it be a continuously long and difficult attempt to limit armaments, establish test bans, and seek through those perilous paths a peaceful world, or will we pile up more and more armaments and play atomic saber-rattling?

A few years ago in the *Saturday Review* there was a series of articles on our desperate attempt to save ourselves through stockpiling of nuclear weapons. It was suggested then that the U.S. possessed the capability of overkilling on a global scale, 125 times; of overkilling the Sino-Soviet area 500 times; and we could overkill the Soviet Union, even allowing for a 50% error, 1250 times.[3] (Overkill is a fascinating term that takes a five-star mind to appreciate.) Is this to be our last word, our ultimate authority? (All of this in the face of Dr. Wiesner's statement—President Kennedy's advisor—that "200 relatively secure missiles would provide an adequate deterrent." In 1963 we had over 940 and by this time these figures have no doubt all been increased many times.) Is this to be our last word—our ultimate authority? A pentagon-like existence, fearfully huddled behind massive stockpiles? Are hydrogen bombs to be the last words?

Or, to change the focus, is materialism to be the last word? Or are racists fearfully paddling into the waters of a lost age to have the last word? Is evil in the world to have the last word? Is our furious attempt to achieve security and material success to be our last word? Are disease and death the last words? Who is to have the last Word? Is man to have it?

II.

Archibald MacLeish in his poetic drama *J.B.*, based on the Book of Job, portrays another kind of cosmic, roaring wind, different from the hydrogen holocaust referred to earlier. MacLeish has a mother and daugh-

ter huddled together after God has addressed J.B. in
the wind:

Jolly Adams: Mother! Mother! What was
               That?
Mrs. Adams: The wind child. Only the wind.
               Only the wind.
Jolly Adams: I heard a word.
Mrs. Adams: You heard the thunder in the wind.
Jolly Adams: Under the wind there was a word . . .[4]

Yes, for the man of faith there is always a *word* in the
cosmic and cataclysmic winds of life. And that Word
belongs to One who is great enough to have the last
or the ultimate Word.

In our Scripture we see the ending of an ageless
book and an ageless problem. The Book of Job is not—
as is often erroneously conceived—about suffering,
but about what is the meaning of faith! Can man
recognize his creatureliness and above all, have faith
in God? Job, like all men, has questions about his
misfortunes, about good and evil, life and death.
Sensing his own righteousness, he quarrels with God
defiantly over his goodness. Our lesson presents us
with an answer—not the answer to Job's questions,
but an entirely different answer. God's answer is in
speaking itself and while it is not the answer Job
expects, there is no longer on the part of God aloof-
ness, indifference, apathy, or estrangement. Job is now
conscious that there is a God who cares for him. God

[97

speaks and Job is confronted in an I-Thou manner. "The bare event of the voice speaking from the whirlwind is a testimony to the love as well as to the greatness of God."[5] God appears and although he changes no question marks into periods, Job learns that God is bent on being God. In a real sense, God is simply teaching Job what he already knew deep within himself.

One portion of the book of Job is a short, important section from the last chapter (42:2-6), where Job—awed by the transcendent voice from the wind—finds his speech again and says to God:

I know that thou canst do all things,
    and that no purpose of thine can be thwarted.
. . . .
Therefore I have uttered what I did not understand,
    things too wonderful for me, which I did not know.
. . . .
I had heard of thee by the hearing of the ear,
    but now my eye sees thee;
therefore, I despise myself,
    and repent in dust and ashes.

In this passage, Job comes to his highest realization—not a glib answer, but an *encounter* which can only be expressed by, "my eye sees thee." As is often the case in biblical religion, he has a sense of sin which accompanies his salvation. And he repents—not from some moral guilt, but from a ruthless and reckless display of distrust in God. In effect, he has now once again found his place as a creature in the cosmic scheme of things and has said in effect, "Thy will be done." He has received awareness, has repented, and finally has received acceptance. God is God; man is man; there is communion based upon grace and faith in the One who is ultimate and who speaks the last and final words.

III.

For the Christian, there is an even deeper disclosure of God's grace, love, and concern. God's Word came another time, in another place, and pictorially also through an earthquake. As his Son was on the cross crying, "My God, my God, why hast thou forsaken me?" he spoke again: "And behold, the curtain of the temple was torn in two, from top to bottom; and the earth shook, and the rocks were split. . . When the centurion and those who were with him, keeping watch over Jesus, saw the earthquake and what took place, they were filled with awe, and said, 'Truly this was a son of God!'" (Matt. 27:51-54).

Yes, God speaks out of the whirlwind and earthquake experiences of life, but he also spoke through a Person—the Word who became flesh, dwelt among us, full of grace and truth. The seemingly impersonal One who sits in judgment on history actually entered history and we beheld his glory. We not only have a

[99

SPLINTERS IN THE QUICK

message such as Job heard, we have the *presence.* A love letter is all right, but it is not the same as when the beloved walks through the door. The Word becomes flesh. The message is incarnated. The voice is given body.

To the Christian, then, the Word is not always in the whirlwind or earthquake, it is sometimes in the still small voice, and above all in God's Son who dramatized the Word in the world. This is the faith of the Christian which looks at the most sordid events realistically, works to redeem them, and knows that the final word is ultimately God's; that behind the catastrophes and cosmic calamities of this or any age stands one whose voice will have the final say.

But to the Christian this is not alone the voice beyond an age in cataclysmic events. To the faithful, the voice in the whirlwind experiences is the same as the still, small voice and can be heard continuously by those who live in faithful trust. The French writer, André Gide decided to stop keeping a journal. All were agog to see what this great man would record as his last entry. It may have seemed anticlimactic to many, for he wrote: "Last words . . . I do not see why one should try to pronounce them louder than the others. At least I do not feel the need of doing so."[6]

No, the last words do not wait until the end of history. They can be heard and trusted now. The Word to be heard then is the same one to be heard now. We sing it rather clumsily in Maltbie D. Babcock's hymn, "This is my Father's world, O let me ne'er forget That though the wrong seems oft so strong, God is the ruler yet." This Word is the one that the faithful Christian hears daily, through the church, the Bible, prayer, and God's action in the world. Therefore, he can live his life apart from the frantic and frenetic anxiety that saps his strength.

The faithful Christian will work hard for the kingdom on earth even though he will be aware that he is often hearing a different drummer than the crowd hears. He will be immersed in life, but will be buoyed constantly by the affirmation that he is not alone, for he has been bought with a price. He lives daily in the faith that God has the final or last Word—not only at the end of history, but even now. As he treads through life's mazes he is assured of God's love, that the Lord of history has revealed himself, has communion with man, and above all, has not only his destiny, but that of history in His hands. This is the faith of the Christian who lives in trusting obedience.

To the Christian, neither Nixon nor Kosygin, NASA nor Nike missiles, the stock market, Elizabeth Arden, nor Mutual Life—none of these has the last word. The last word is his whom the poet Lowell describes: "behind the dim unknown, Standeth God within the shadow, keeping watch above his own."

It is this kind of faith and this kind of living which the outstanding Cambridge historian Herbert Butterfield described in an analogy which dramatizes the

[101

faith a Christian has in a God who is sovereign, and who therefore ultimately speaks the last word:

"We might say that this human story is like a piece of orchestral music that we are playing over for the first time. In our presumption we may act as though we were the composer of the piece or try to bring out our own particular part as the leading one. But in reality I personally see only the part of, shall we say, the second clarinet and of course even within the limits of that I never know what is coming after the page that now lies open before me. None of us can know what the whole score amounts to except as far as we have already played it over together, and even so the meaning of a passage may not be clear all at once. . . . If I am sure that B flat is the next note that I have to play I can never feel certain that it will not come with surprising implications until I have heard what the other people are going to play at the same moment. And no single person in the orchestra can have any idea when or where this piece is going to end.

"But we can have faith that the composer of the piece will help us sound the last chord in a final harmony."[7]

The Lost
Parable

The Lost Parable

Luke 15:1-10

Two parables from the 15th chapter of Luke furnish
the Gospel lesson for the ninth Sunday after Pente-
cost. And, frankly, they trouble me. Here again, as
so often in the Gospels, it seems the good guys take
it on the chin. Those in the white hats—ourselves of
course—come out on the short end, for the point
seems to be that heaven rejoices over that *one* who
is lost rather than the ninety-nine good sheep. Or that
one coin seems more important than the other nine.
"Rejoice, for I have found the coin that was lost."
And, again, there is exceeding joy over that *one* who
repents.

Many times we resent these slaps at goodness.
St. Leo Durocher is right! "Nice guys seem to finish

last." You remember the parable of the workers in the vineyard who came out at 4:30 in the afternoon after sitting around all day? They were paid as much as those who had started work at dawn. The gospel seems so unfair at times, doesn't it? All this fuss over the lost, the sinners—not much to be said for the saved and the saints. It reminds me of the mountaineer who remarked after he had returned from Europe after World War I, "I shore wisht I'd seen Paris before I was converted." The sinners seem to have all the fun and get the rewards too, even in the Gospels.

I.

Let us look closer at the stories in Luke 15. The first one tells of the one sheep lost and the pains endured to recover it. (Here in the Southwest, change that sheep to a steer and we see it vividly.) The coin—like the pearl of great price—deserves a thorough search. In both of these stories there is something *lost*—a *search*—and a *joy* in finding—a kind of three-stage rocket of salvation.

And it is this pattern that has been the church's stance throughout history, particularly in her evangelism. We have talked about the lost souls, the necessity of saving them in the name of God who loves sinners. We have become accustomed to this. We sing about the ninety and nine that safely lay in the

shelter of the fold and the one out on the hills away—
on the mountains wild and bare, away from the tender Shepherd's care. But after the Shepherd had gone
to the desert and found his sheep, there arose the
glad cry, "Rejoice I have found my sheep. Rejoice
the Lord brings back his own." This image is familiar
to most of us. We feel comfortable with this concept
of the church's work. This theme of lost sinners and
God's love for them sending us out is something
we all understand.

And we shouldn't minimize this role of the Christian
and the church. Sinner may be an old-fashioned word,
but lostness is not. Lost is a modern word, along with
alienation, estrangement. There are plenty of lost
today. And we cannot minimize the "lostness" of the
"lost." Only one who has known the pain of separation
can know the depths of lostness—estrangement—from
God and others. So we understand the lost sheep and
the lost coin and we see that these parables tell us
that our attitude toward these lost is crucial. It is the
nature of God's love to be seeking. Here is the key to
the parable.

It is interesting to remember that in John's Gospel
Jesus himself is referred to as the Good Shepherd.
"I am the good shepherd; . . . I lay down my life for
the sheep" (John 10:14-15). So we understand the
parables of lostness, of seeking and finding, and re-
joicing.

[107

II.

But we have a problem in our day finding the lost. Where are these lost? It is very difficult to pinpoint the "outsider." J. B. Phillips refers to tax-collectors and "disreputable folk" as the outsiders who came to hear Jesus.[1] But, today the outsider is often "inside." And what does it mean to be "outside" anyway? In our day, the church's attitude toward the outsider is changing, and thus the mission of the church is changing. We now think of the people outside the church in terms of identifying with them rather than saving them. After all, Jesus' justification for being with sinners and tax collectors is the basis for these parables. The church is living with outsiders—is identifying with them and with the world. We are seeing that the church is a mission church—not so much bringing people in, but going out and giving itself for the world. Jesus didn't come to save the church, after all, but the world.

We hear much of the generation gap. Recently I heard a speaker tell that in the secular university the church is *out* with the students, but Jesus is *in*. The young people say he put his body where his words were. Is this what the church in mission does? Further, we find that the separation between the church and the world is too rigid. God does his work in the world as well as in the church. Karl Rahner talks about the anonymous Christian, meaning that the person outside the church may really be a Christian anonymously. If so, our mission is not to "save" him but to witness to that faith already there and stand alongside him.

III.

The real problem, though, in locating the lost is trying to distinguish between the "outsider" and the "insider." And here is where the parables get pointed, for perhaps we ourselves are the lost. We have problems relating the characters in the Bible to ourselves. Jesus' audience, for instance. Tax collectors and sinners. Us or not? The scribes and Pharisees as the onlookers. Us or not? The lost sheep and the lost coin. Us or not? The woman searching or the Shepherd seeking. Us or not? The problem lies at the point where the outsider becomes the insider. That's why it is difficult to talk about the church and the outsiders. We are they. Someone has said that the church is not a refuge for saints but a hospital for sinners. We are out in mission not to show off our piety, but as beggars telling other beggars where to get bread, as D. T. Niles put it.

And, so, in our most honest moments, we have to admit it—aren't we the lost ourselves? fearful? prejudiced? alienated? You see these parables are for us. We are torn apart personally. For each one of us is possessed by fears, insecurities, prejudices, hates that rend our personalities and make us less than whole.

What about our families? Someone has said that there are Berlin walls in American homes. Is that true?

Or our communities: Aren't we really frightened and "lost" concerning our racial problems, the population explosion, space, air and water pollution, and war? These great imponderables make us feel anxious, worried, alone, alienated, and lost.

It is at this precise point that our "lostness" becomes our salvation. And then these parables speak to us. They are really good news, for they are telling us that God loves us and seeks us. That's not pious drivel. That's good news of cosmic consequences—that the Great Creator loves us and seeks us.

IV.

But, you say, "How do we really know? I may be a sheep or a coin in the parable, but that doesn't mean much to me." So it doesn't. And here the scene shifts radically, for there is something needed to complete the picture. And what is needed is the lost passage—the one not mentioned in today's lesson. The forgotten story is the one that doesn't appear, it is the one that makes the chapter come alive. It is, of course, the parable of the prodigal son (vv. 11-32) and it is introduced almost as an afterthought. Most versions of the Bible introduce this parable as the RSV does, simply, "And he said . . ." Only Moffatt changes the emphasis and then but slightly—"He *also* said."[2] That might be the most important *also* in all history, for as one theologian has said, the prodigal son story dramatizes the entire Christian gospel. However that may be, it is certainly the parable that makes sense out of this whole chapter, for it completes it and dramatizes what seeking love is all about. We move from sheep and coins to people here.

A comparable parable to the parable of the sheep appears in Matthew 18:12-14 in which there is a significant difference in the seekers after the sheep. In Matthew, the shepherd goes out and says "if" he finds it. In Luke the shepherd goes out "until" he finds the sheep. This is the kind of love which is dramatized in the parable of the prodigal.

In this parable we see on one side the younger son —the generation gap—the traditional view of the sinner, the lost, the outsider (the publican and the sinner). But on the other side we are also shown the elder brother, the "insider" who is lost—that's us (the scribes and Pharisees). The elder son lived closer to the father than the younger son—yet he was really farther away than his kid brother.

The focus of the story is really the father, the prodigal father I call him, whose love was spilled out, wasted, thrown away. This is more than a shepherd untangling a sheep, or a housewife sweeping for a coin. Here is a father going out to the gate and enfolding the son in his arms. One of the most beautiful lines in all literature is this one: "While he was yet at a distance. . . ." Not merely waiting, but rushing out, seeking, forgiving, spilling over in love.

This is the kind of love we see in the Good Shepherd and in the Cross. When we see the Cross, it is difficult to know all it means, but we sing:

> Were the whole realm of nature mine,
> That were an offering far too small
> Love so amazing, so divine,
> Demands my life, my soul, my all.

Here is the meaning of these parables: God seeking the lost—and finding—and that's us.

One more thing, though. If we are the lost, too, of the parable—if we have been sought and found—what do we do? Well, we go out—not to get scalps, but to live these new lives in celebration in the world and to stand shoulder to shoulder with others in the world, witnessing to God and for his humanity. We, too, like our Lord may put our bodies where our words are, for it was said of him that God was in him reconciling (get that word) the world (not the church) unto himself.

One Thing
Is Needed

One Thing Is Needed

Luke 10:38-42; 12:22-31

One of the most poignant and tender stories of the New Testament comes from Luke 10. It tells of Jesus' visit to the home of Martha and Mary at Bethany and is replete with the warmth of Jesus' humanity—his dealings with human beings. Perhaps it is significant that this little episode is sandwiched between two more familiar and perhaps more theological passages: that of the Good Samaritan and that of Jesus' giving of the Lord's Prayer to his disciples. For in this simple story we sense the heartbeat and earthiness of our Lord's dealings with ordinary human beings.

The story is simple. It is a visit to the home of Martha and Mary—the sisters of Lazarus. Martha is busy with her household tasks, especially those of serving the honored guest. Mary sits at the feet of the Master, listening eagerly to his teaching. Martha becomes so distracted by the serving that she chides her sister by asking Jesus to tell Mary to help. Jesus responds with characteristic warmth and tenderness— yet putting the problem in its proper perspective. "Martha, Martha, you are anxious and troubled about many things; *one thing is needful.* Mary has chosen the good portion, which shall not be taken away from her." In this mild rebuke Jesus cuts through the details of the narrative and gives a message which speaks to our present day.

Perhaps we, too, can learn something of cosmic importance by seeing through the homey details to the point of the story. For the sisters represent all of us in certain ways, and perhaps by looking at each more closely, we can see our own lives in relation to the *one thing needed in our Christian experience.*

I.

The major person of the story is undoubtedly Mary. She chose the good portion. Some might want to suggest that she was not a good housekeeper or that perhaps she was lazy, more content to sit and visit than to attend to the menial tasks of householding. Someone else might say that she didn't sense the seriousness of the situation, that she didn't sense the importance of the guest. That in the company of Jesus, the Master, she was unconcerned for his comfort. Or that she was more concerned for the contemplative life, rather than the life of service or the life of action.

But, to take these views would be to do an injustice to the narrative. Jesus relates that Mary rather than neglecting a duty, chose the highest good. She was able in a moment of tremendous portent—in the presence of the Master—to choose the most significant course. She sat at the feet of the Master. "One thing is needful" and she chose it. This one thing was to know him intimately, to heed his teachings, to seek his kingdom.

A little later we see the importance of this concept reiterated when Jesus admonished his disciples not to be anxious about their lives, or about what they should eat or drink. The birds of the air and the lilies of the field teach us a lesson in terms of their faith and lack of anxious concern. Instead of seeking that which the nations of the world would seek, Jesus tells his disciples to seek his kingdom and all these things will be theirs as well.

Here then is the *one* thing needful which Mary chose. In the midst of all life, the one thing most important of all was the relationship to the Master, his teachings, his kingdom. Now, do these words have any value to us in our twentieth century? Can modern people really take seriously the admonition that only *one* thing is needful—seeking the kingdom of God? Think of that, one thing—our relationship to God is *the* important thing in our life.

[117

If we were to list the priorities of our lives, the kingdom of God and his righteousness might not be too high on our list. We live in a world of different values. We want success; we want social standing; we want education; we want money; we want a successful business; we want a fine family; we want a fine home; we want a nice car. These are the items, which lead all the rest. The things of the spirit come far down the list for most moderns. We fit God into our scheme of things, or perhaps in time of trouble we seek him; but he is seldom *the* reality we seek.

And, yet, in our most honest moments, we too, like Mary *know* that there is one thing needed. In times when all of life's ornaments are stripped away, we stand before the one great reality of life and acknowledge him to be the center of our life. For it is only God who can stand when the winds of transiency blow away what we consider important.

A business executive walks from a doctor's office where he has been told that he has a year to live. The fact that he has an income of $50,000 a year and a successful business is to no avail. Yesterday, they were the most important things in the world. Today, his sense of values has changed completely and he would literally give everything, yes, give everything away to have heard another verdict. At a time like this he seeks the one thing. Yesterday, God may have been far down the list; today he is everything. Yes, in times of tragedy—the loss of a loved one, the rebellion of a child, the broken home—life is placed in perspective and we seek the one thing needed in which to center our lives.

But, if the lesson is valid it must be valid for other times, too. Here is another man. He happens to be a successful executive, too. But he has chosen the best part early in life. He knows that there is only one who is unchanging, one who is big enough to demand all of our loyalties. And here he has placed his trust. His life, home, and family are oriented around the spiritual verities and faith in God. His loyalties are not divided. Therefore, he can see his life, his job, as a stewardship from God. Anxiety, fears, the constant revolving-door existence are kept in check. Not that he is not confronted with crises, but he has chosen the best portion and his life is secure in that basic trust in God.

Yes, from Mary we get the truth which is eternal. In the midst of the activity of life, one thing is needed. Not that we are to neglect or despise the activities of the world. Remember, Jesus reminded his disciples to seek the kingdom and these things would be placed in perspective. Still, seek the kingdom of God and his righteousness. This is the good portion; this is the one needful thing.

II.

But if we learn so much from Mary in the story, is

[119

there some positive truth that can be learned from Martha?

Certainly, on the surface, Martha does not come out too well. And she has received her judgment through the years. In the midst of activity, she lost sight of the major goal. In the company of the Master, she was busy with lesser things. But there is a human quality here which makes Martha understandable to most of us. On the more literal level, we too would be concerned if an important guest was coming. The cleaning woman would come in, perhaps a cateress, and perhaps the hostess would be too tired to enjoy the fellowship with the honored guest.

Or, figuratively, we too are so engrossed in the activities of life that the main objective somehow slips into anonymity. Like Tithonus in Greek mythology who was turned into a grasshopper, we may become little Tithonuses hopping through life but missing the central facts.

Yet there is a quality in the character of Martha which speaks of something warm, human, and true. Remember that Jesus' rebuke was mild and gentle. He senses the graciousness, the desire to please, the concern for another's welfare.

If we turn to John's Gospel we see Martha in still another light—that of a woman who has learned, who has become perceptive, who has sensed the importance of the Master in her life. You remember the story of Lazarus whom Jesus raised from the dead? When Jesus was a way off, Martha ran to him and said,

"Lord, if you had been here, my brother would not have died." "I believe that you are the Christ, the son of God, he who is coming into the world" (John 11:21, 27). A long way from the earlier episode. Here it is Martha who sensed that Jesus was in a unique relationship to God, that he was actually the Lord not only of her life but of all life. What a tremendous insight for anyone to make—especially the one who had missed the mark at an earlier time.

Martha's qualities are still valuable today. For example, we can think of the importance of the life of service as over against the purely introspective Christian life. We are to be active Christians; life is not only a personal, subjective road to salvation, but our Christian life has ramifications in regard to our neighbors and brothers in the name of Christian service. Martha showed this concern, and that Christian virtue is to be ours, too.

On the purely homey level, there is a truth here in regard to the earthy, human, daily tasks of life. There is a Christian virtue in homemaking, in the day-to-day life that most of us lead, that God can be served in the day-to-day tasks and that these tasks can be meaningful when seen in their proper relationships. All husbands no doubt feel like singing what Archibald MacLeish wrote to his wife:

> In all that becomes a woman
> Her words and her ways are beautiful

Love's lovely duty,
The well-swept room

Wherever she is there is sun
And time and a sweet air
Peace is there,
Work done

There are always curtains and flowers
And candles and baked bread
And a cloth spread
And a clean house[1]

Yes, there is a God-given quality about the kind of devotion which loses itself in the ordinary tasks of life. Or to put it another way, the ordinary tasks which most of us perform can take on a new meaning when brought under the love and concern of God.

If there is a message to be carried away, it is probably to be found in the blending of these two personalities in our Scripture lesson. For there is truth here that none of us can escape.

We can reiterate our faith that there is only one thing needful in our lives. No activity, no desire, no ambition, should obscure the good portion which stands when all else has vanished. "Seek ye *first* the kingdom of God," and all these other things will be added unto you—will be put into proper perspective (Matt. 6:33).

We can also affirm that God is in our daily lives,

closer than hands and feet, never far from any one of us. Our lives do have meaning; they are trusts from God. We are stewards and our jobs are callings, places where we can witness to his love and concern. And no job, however trivial, need shut us off from his gracious love. These words of Brother Lawrence bring this truth home to us. He who labored in the kitchen of the monastery could write:

> The time of business does not with me differ from the time of prayer, and in the noise and clatter of my kitchen, while several persons are at the same time calling for different things, I possess God in a great tranquility as if I were upon my knees at the Blessed Sacrament.[2]

Here, then, is the Christian blending necessary for a whole life. To combine the spiritual with the active. To sense the place of God in our lives and then to embody his will in our lives and daily tasks: life of solitude, life of service; life of inspiration, life of perspiration; life of spirituality, life of actuality.

Most of us won't find ourselves performing such menial tasks, but these lines of a simple English maid of 19 express a deep truth:

Although I must have Martha's hands, I have a Mary
   mind
And when I black the boots and shoes, Thy sandals,
   Lord, I find

[123

I think of how they trod the earth, what time I scrub
the floor;
Accept this meditation, Lord, I haven't time for more.[3]

What greater summary could we have for this simple
biblical incident—indeed what better summary for the
whole of the Christian life: the hands of Martha, the
mind of Mary.

Jesus
and the Generation Gap

Jesus and the Generation Gap

Luke 2:39-52

One morning, a couple of years ago, I woke up and discovered that we had a teen-ager in the house. The shock of this discovery became evident when I was told, "Dad, we just must begin to do something about those white shirts; you've got to get those sideburns down a bit, and for heaven sakes, let's get rid of those somber, baggy suits." Occasionally I've had to leave my books and go sit through some Simon and Garfunkel, Fifth Dimension, music from Hair, and be urged to listen to the words as much as the music or beat. Some changes have occurred, even though I'm still not very good hippie material. But, with her help, I find that although the generation gap is real, there can be some communication if the lines are open and there is a willingness to listen.

What I have been describing could, I am sure, be duplicated in hundreds of homes and Christian families all over the country—with varying results. The fact of the generation gap is so much of a truism in our day as to be self-evident and even a cliché. The reason we are giving it attention today is not to analyze and discuss the cleavage between youth and adults (remembering that both of these terms cannot be described entirely in terms of age). The simple fact is that the Gospel lesson for the third Sunday in Epiphany—whatever else it is talking about—seems to suggest that here is a generation gap and, of all places, in the life of Jesus.

I.

This little vignette in the second chapter of Luke is significant for it is the one scrap of Scripture which purports to talk about the early life of Jesus. Sandwiched between the birth narratives and the beginning of his public ministry, the author was obviously endeavoring to show that the Incarnation was real. Writing as he did after the Resurrection events, and remembering the stories of Jesus' miraculous birth, Luke was obviously trying to combat the heresy that Jesus was only divine and that his earthly life was a charade, chimerical at best—a shadowplay with the human barely covering the divine nature that was playing out an already determined cosmic drama.

Luke was combating what the theologians call the docetic heresy which taught that in the person of Jesus the human only seemed to be real, that he was divinity walking around in not so thinly disguised human form.

So it is significant that here we find an almost utterly human story devoid of divine connotations. It begins and ends with telling of Jesus' growth in strength, wisdom, and favor with God and man—a story without supernatural portents and told with simplicity and restraint. It can only demonstrate from the details Jesus' early interest in religion. To see this incident in perspective we must remind ourselves that not all of the stories about Jesus that circulated in the early church were so filled with human simplicity. The Apocryphal New Testament is filled with stories which make him a divine wonder-worker, even from the first. He is a combination of the Batman's young friend Robin, Jack Armstrong, and Superman. In the Gospel of Thomas (a book dating in one version no earlier than the sixth century and in another the thirteenth), Jesus at five years old made sparrows out of clay, made them come alive, and sold them in the streets. Although he was divine, this version has him pretty angry most of the time. Anyone who angered him was struck blind, or dead. His father once twisted his ear and Jesus bawled him out good and proper. All his teachers became his servants, he raised the dead when he felt like it, and was a precocious wonder-worker

[129

who soon manifested his divine nature by these feats of exciting legerdemain.

To turn from the apocryphal legends and look at this simple story in Luke makes Jesus seem considerably closer to us, humanly speaking, than he does in most places in the Gospel record. Jesus accompanied his parents to Jerusalem to attend the feast of the Passover when he was twelve years old. After the great holiday was over, Jesus stayed behind and, interestingly, the parents didn't even know it. There's a generation gap right there. After three days they returned to look for him and found him in the Temple. That, too, is designed to cause estrangement. Can you imagine a father taking off for San Francisco to look for his son? His first stop would not be Grace Cathedral, Episcopal, but Haight-Ashbury. Jesus' very concern for religion might have been one element in the division between himself and parents.

And what about teachers? Does that sound like a generation-gap theme? Here was Jesus sitting in the Temple, listening to the rabbis and, heaven forbid, questioning them. And they were all amazed at his answers. Now the parents were astonished, perhaps angry, and certainly parental—in being self-centered. Why have you treated *us* so? *We* have been anxious! About his lostness? Their injured pride? Maybe even his public display! Jesus' reply about being in his father's house really threw them a curve. They did not understand either what he was doing there and certainly not his enigmatic language. Does that sound familiar to any of you? Yet, strangely enough, he went home with them—evidently not in pique—and was even obedient to them. Then the curtain falls.

We could leave the story there and have a parallel in biblical terms which is amazing in its contemporaneity. We could all "tune in" or "turn on" at appropriate places in the story and draw some conclusions concerning our parents, our teachers, ourselves. We could have the feeling that the Bible is amazingly relevant and that the generation gap is certainly nothing new. But to stop there would be both an injustice to the biblical incident and a failure to see what the true dimension of the generation gap is all about, then and now. Thus, we need a replay. We need to run the story through again and see an entirely different dimension to it.

II.

What we are talking about is only the generation gap on the surface. What is really at stake in this story—and ours—is *authority*. Keeping that in mind as we look at this narrative will give us the insight that permeates the biblical faith and places in perspective our own failures to relate to one another.

Jesus in the story represents youth with his estrangement from parents, his confrontation with teachers, his searching inquiry into the meaning of things. We

[131

must always be careful, however, when we define youth solely in age terms. Richard Poirier resists defining youth at all because "it refers to the rare human condition of exuberance, expectation, impulsiveness, and above all, of freedom from believing that all the so-called 'necessities' of life and thought are in fact necessities."[1] This does not limit youth to the young, for older people can fit this description of youth; and there are also those chronologically young people who are completely fossilized. But here Jesus is—as youth —in conflict with his parents, challenging the authority of the teachers. The new student generation—an early version!

Some of us have tried to have a sympathetic ear in regard to the younger generation, even to the consternation of some of our peers who feel we may be "selling out" if we endeavor to relate and communicate. But deep in our hearts we know that young people are right in many ways. They are probably smarter than our generation and we resent it. They feel much more deeply about things, and we rather resent that too. Perhaps even secretly we're jealous of our lost youth. This does not mean that we can always identify with the young, but we can try to communicate. We can accept—even though critically.

Normally, however, we want them to grow up— and we mean by that for them to become like we are. For some, it means that girls should get through school, marry a nice, solid young man, and move to the suburbs in a ranch-style, three bedroom home with a wall-to-wall mortgage, and begin the humdrum living of many adults. A recent cartoon showed two coeds talking and one was saying, "I just want an average, normal, happy life: love, marriage, a home, children . . . separation, divorce, love, marriage, a home, children . . ." For the young men, it is to settle down, get over this idealistic business, and get to work. "Why have you treated us so?" we older people say. "We have been so anxious about you. Be like us." In the movie *The Graduate*, the hero responds to the pats on the back and the inquiries of his parents' friends —"What are you going to do?" "Going into business?" "When are you going to get started?" "When are you beginning?" "What are you going to be?"—by muttering, "I just want to be a little different," and receives blank stares. Get over the childishness and grow up!

The reason so many young people hesitate to do that is that they see us and our generation all too clearly to want to join us. They see us needing a couple of highballs after work before we can have dinner, they watch us around April 15 with real financial mystification. They wonder about our insensitivity to the morality of war and the ethical questions involved in ecology and pollution, and they throw up their hands in horror. One astute observer of today's scene says that the youth are not immoral and nihilistic at all, but really quite moral and even puritan. He cites as proof their concern about war, pollution, and the quite open way they talk about love and sex. Our generation seems to be cautious about the first issues, and secretly worked out the last in the back seats of 1939 Fords.

But let's not be too hard on my generation. Actually we had our rebellion. But it was programmed for us—it was called World War II. Maybe you read about it. It was in all the papers at the time. We didn't have to rebel toward our own as much, for we had a symbol of antipathy to drain off most of our hates—we called it Nazism. And, since World War II the specter of communism has also programmed to a certain extent our rebellious instincts. And, so the youth must be understanding of us—the exciting wines of life have been changed to water for many of us as we face age, job disillusionments, bad marriages, and mortality.

Now all that we have been saying in regard to parents and children could also be said here about the generation gap between students and teachers. Evidently one existed in this story, even though the famous picture of the boy Jesus confounding the elders in the Temple is probably not correctly labeled "Jesus Teaching in the Temple," but should be "Jesus Learning in the Temple." In education, the present student generation demands, with some justification, an education which is meaningful—which is relevant. Questionings, dialogs, confrontations, sit-ins, even riots are the outward and sometimes painful expressions of the inner sacrament of concern that what is called education might be just that. This calls all prerogatives into question, and faculties feel faint at heart when their own frailties become so exposed. Some, of course, have responded, have changed, have adapted, have communicated, recognizing that the new confrontation is threatening, but exciting too, and more honest when relationships that are truly mutually edifying can be established.

But I don't want to suggest that the youth are always right and the oldsters wrong. Many youths feel deeply, but to no apparent purpose. Many will question and rebel, but irresponsibly. And all older people are not petrified—either by fear or texture. What we need to see is that there should be in our lives something transcendent to all of us which unites us as we give our allegiance to something greater than ourselves. For when people give themselves to something outside themselves they are coming to terms with their own misplaced authority.

See this passage again! When his parents asked what he was doing in the Temple, he reminded them that he must be about his Father's business. This is not just a rebellious youth running away from home, jousting with rabbis, and repudiating parents. Jesus is seeking a proper authority, transcending both self and parents, as his highest allegiance, and that was God. It is no wonder they don't understand. They still don't. All through Jesus' earthly ministry he was constantly confronted by this business of "by what authority do you do these things: teaching, healing, preaching?" "Tell us by what authority you do these things?" or "Who is it that gave you this authority?" And the answer, of course, is obvious: Jesus found his authority in God, and that changed the perspective and allegiance in his life. So it is no wonder that his parents did not understand him when he used the word "Father" in front of them, but applied it to someone else. For when he called God "Father," he changed his relationship not only to his own parents, but to himself as well and seized a new authority for his life.

Later on in the Book of Luke (chapter 8) Jesus' mother and brothers tried to contact him when he was teaching, but could not get to him for the crowd. When he was told that his mother and brothers were outside he told them, "My mother and brothers are those who hear the word of God and do it." This seems cruel, but he was lifting the concept of filial relationships right into the realm of *universal family*. He did not love his parents less, he simply put his life—and theirs—in perspective by choosing an authority which transcended both.

Thus, there is no contradiction in his going back to Nazareth with his parents and being obedient to them. He had found his ultimate loyalty and although it broadened his concept of family, it did not destroy his relations with his parents. Indeed, it probably made them more meaningful. He had found the center of his life, his future was clear—he increased in wisdom, stature, and in favor with God and man. So, metaphorically speaking, he closed the gap between himself and God and consequently between himself and parents and other men. When he found his authority, the controlling center of his life, then all these other things were put into perspective. The gaps were bridged with proper authority.

III.

All of this says something to us as we go into our several worlds with all their gaps—generational and otherwise. For one thing, we all—whatever age—need to get over the idea, which is idolatrous, that our ultimate authority is in ourselves, our parents, our teachers, our nation, our sweethearts, or even our married partners. No human being or institution deserves that kind of idolatrous worship. Yet, when we have the right kind of authority in our lives, then we are free to relate meaningfully to the ones we may be estranged from, precisely because our own lives are clarified in their purpose. Youth are right to rebel against authoritarianism and paternalism; they need an authority big enough, though, to give meaning and purpose to their lives. And so do parents: they need to quit trying to find their fulfillment in each other, their children, or their jobs, and realize their own "uptightness" is due to this fuzzy authority in their lives. We need to be able to say "Tom, you're in the twilight of a mediocre career," or, "John, you are looking down the short end of the barrel," and depend upon our faith in God to relieve our "hang-ups."

As Christians we affirm, interestingly enough, that this boy Jesus who grew in wisdom, stature, and favor with God ended up bridging the generation gap (both of *age* and *ages*) with a cross—of all things. A funny kind of bridge. We Christians affirm that when we see that cross we have an authority that frees us from our "hang-ups" and lets us be ourselves with an allegiance that gives a real authority to our lives and takes away the frantic and frenetic searching for lesser gods around which to orient our lives.

Thus, we hope that youth are going to move in to adulthood with an authority to give purpose. Oh, I hope they will not leave their youthful idealism, which one person calls poetry (the dreams of youth) in contrast to prose (which is real life). Says Ignazio Silone, of becoming adult, "The poetry is over and the prose has begun."[2] We hope there can be poetry, too, in our lives right through to the end. But they will take their place responsibly when their authority is clear. It will not be my generation's style, thank God, but it will be a commitment to the poetry of youth, tempered by the prose of age. And even they can go home to parents with joy, maybe even referring to mother once again in words which Conrad Richter puts in the mouth of one of his characters as that "tender rock in gingham."[3]

For when we find that transcendent authority we find a center which diminishes the concern for the circumferences of life and permits us to work for racial betterment, ecological causes, moral issues—all of these with a calmness and program derived from this very authority itself. Indeed, some of the youth—and adults—may even find their way back to the church as they find that authority—if they have left or are leaving. W. H. Auden, one who began with the church, lost it, and then returned, recently remarked that "there's a great deal of difference in believing something *still* and believing it *again*."[4] When you appropriate it for yourself and not by heredity, it is going to be yours.

Maybe what we're trying to say is that when the focus is on the highest authority these lesser authorities are placed in perspective. Yet, strangely enough, we are brought closer together not only by the One whom we Christians believe bridged that gap, but by the very fact that our specific focus on the Authority above all authorities brings us at last to the same task.

In New York City on a subway wall was scrawled: "Christ is the answer." Someone had drawn a line through that and had written below: "What was the question?" The question was and continues to be, where is the ultimate authority in your life? When that is answered, then the gaps—generational or otherwise—will be bridged!

Source Notes

Unidentified Objects

1. Arthur Miller, *Death of a Salesman, New Voices in the American Theater* (New York: The Modern Library, 1955), p. 225.

2. Oscar F. Blackwelder, *The Interpreter's Bible*, Vol. 10 (Nashville: Abingdon-Cokesbury, 1953), p. 530.

3. Raymond T. Stamm, ibid.

4. Nathan A. Scott, Jr., *Modern Literature and the Religious Frontier* (New York: Harper & Brothers, 1958), p. 93.

5. Carson McCullers, *The Member of the Wedding, Critics' Choice* (New York: Hawthorn Books, 1955), Act I, p. 471.

6. Robert Browning, quoted in *The Interpreter's Bible*, op. cit., p. 92.

What's in a Name?

1. William Shakespeare, *Romeo and Juliet*, Act II, Scene 2.

2. Nikos Kazantzakis, *The Greek Passion* (New York: Simon and Schuster, 1954).

3. "Intelligence Report," *Parade*, May 16, 1965.

4. Newspaper clipping, Associated Press, London, England, undated.

5. James Joyce, *A Portrait of the Artist as a Young Man* (New York: The Viking Press, 1956), p. 12.

6. "Name," *The Interpreter's Dictionary of the Bible*, Vol. III (New York: Abingdon Press, 1962), p. 502.

7. J. D. Salinger, *Franny and Zooey* (Boston: Little, Brown & Co., 1955), p. 39.

8. William R. Mueller, *The Prophetic Voice in Modern Fiction* (New York: Association Press, 1959), p. 30.

9. N. Richard Nash, *The Rainmaker* (New York: Random House, 1955), Act II, p. 131. Copyright © 1955 by N. Richard Nash. Reprinted by permission of Random House, Inc.

10. Ibid., p. 134.

Anyone for Shepherding?

1. James A. Weschler, *Newsweek*, March 22, 1965.

2. Kazantzakis, p. 256.

3. Georgia Harkness, "The Agony of God," *The Glory of God* (Nashville: Abingdon-Cokesbury, 1943), p. 16.

4. Francois Mauriac, *The Lamb* (New York: Farrar, Straus and Cudahy, 1955), p. 95.

Tragedy and Triumph

1. Quoted in *The Saturday Review*.

2. Quoted in *The Nashville Tennessean*, November 23, 1958.

3. Jean-Paul Sartre, *No Exit and Three Other Plays* (New York: Vintage Books, 1955), p. 47.

4. John B. Dykes.

5. Godfrey Fox Bradby, quoted in A. M. Hunter, *Intro-*

ducing New Testament Theology (London: SCM Press, Ltd., 1957), p. 24.

6. Winston Churchill, *Triumph and Tragedy* (Boston: Houghton Mifflin Co., 1953), p. v.

Two Minutes Till Midnight

1. *The New English Bible, New Testament* (New York: Oxford University Press, New York: Cambridge University Press, 1961).

2. *The Bible: An American Translation. The New Testament,* Edgar T. Goodspeed, trans. (Chicago: University of Chicago Press, 1935).

3. J. B. Phillips, *The New Testament in Modern English* (New York: The Macmillan Company, 1958).

4. Hermann Hagedorn, *The Bomb That Fell on America* (New York: Association Press, 1948), p. 44. Used by permission of Mrs. Hermann Hagedorn.

5. Albert Camus, *The Fall,* (New York: Alfred A. Knopf, 1959), p. 70.

And the Walls Came Tumbling Down

1. Robert Frost, *Come In and Other Poems* (New York: Henry Holt and Co., 1943), p. 74.

The Last Word

1. T. S. Eliot, "The Hollow Men," *Collected Poems 1909–1962* (New York: Harcourt Brace Jovanovich, Inc., 1963).

2. Reprinted by permission of The World Publishing Company from *The Last Word* by James Broughton. Copyright © 1958 by James Broughton. From the collection entitled *Religious Drama 3* edited by Marvin Halverson, pp. 21; 27. Copyright © 1959 by The World Publishing Company.

3. *Saturday Review,* May 4, 1963.

4. Archibald MacLeish, *J. B.* (Boston: Houghton Mifflin Co., 1958), pp. 130-31.

5. Samuel Terrien, *The Interpreter's Bible*, Vol. 3, p. 1173.

6. Andre Gide, quoted in *The Interpreter's Bible*.

7. Herbert Butterfield, *Christianity and History* (London: G. Bell, 1949), p. 94.

The Lost Parable

1. Mark 2:15, 16, J. B. Phillips, *The New Testament in Modern English* (New York: The Macmillan Co., 1958).

2. James Moffatt, *A New Translation of the Bible* (New York: Harper & Brothers, 1935).

One Thing Is Needed

1. Archibald MacLeish, "Poem in Prose," *Actfive* (New York: Random House, 1948). "Poem in Prose" is copyright 1948 by Archibald MacLeish. Reprinted by permission of Random House, Inc.

2. Brother Lawrence, *The Practice of the Presence of God* (New York: Fleming Revell, n.d.), p. 25.

3. "The Divine Office of the Kitchen," attributed to Cecily R. Hallack.

Jesus and the Generation Gap

1. Richard Poirier, "War Against the Young," *Atlantic* 222:55-64, p. 64.

2. Ignazio Silone, *Bread and Wine* (New York: New American Library, 1946), p. 122.

3. Conrad Richter, *A Simple Honorable Man* (New York: Alfred A. Knopf, 1962), p. 109.

4. Jon Bradshaw, "Holding to Schedule with W. H. Auden," *Esquire*, January 1970, p. 138.